Disc...
North...
and
The Broads

by
Debbie Bartlett

Leading Edge™
press and publishing

in association with

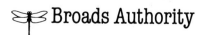
Broads Authority

Published by Leading Edge Press & Publishing Ltd,
The Old Chapel, Burtersett, Hawes, North Yorkshire, DL8
3PB.
☎ (0969) 667566

A CIP Catalogue record for this book is available from the British Library.

ISBN 0 948135 31 X

Series Editor Stan Abbott
Production Editor J R Taylor
Designed by Tim Wright
Sketch maps by Nick Bagguley
Colour reprographics by Impression, Leeds
Printed and bound in Great Britain by Ebenezer Baylis & Son Ltd, Worcester

* The maps which accompany the walks in this book are for guidance only. The publishers strongly recommend that walkers also carry the relevant Ordnance Survey sheet.

Title page illustration: Pleasure wherry Hathor, *a living and working example of Broads history*

Contents

Foreword

IN 1989, the Norfolk and Suffolk Broads became Britain's newest national park, in all but name. Although some of us had been working to protect and enhance the very special Broads landscape for some years before that, this was the year that Parliament passed legislation that gave us responsibility for addressing some of the problems facing a fragile landscape without direct comparison anywhere else in Britain, or Europe.

Since then, I would like to think that our administration has done much to halt the decline of the waterways that make the Broads so special and, indeed, to reverse that process. We have also worked hard to ensure, not only that the public can enjoy the broads, rivers and marshes, but that people may do so in a way which does not harm the sensitive environment.

To that end, this book by Debbie Bartlett, so finely illustrated by Richard Denyer, represents another step forward. We are fortunate in the Broads to still possess a network of local rail services that criss-cross the area, and Debbie has shown how these can be used, often in conjunction with the use of boats on the Broads themselves, by people who either do not have access to a car or who have chosen to break free from the constraints that using our vehicles can impose when we want to explore the countryside.

The extra dimension of the North Norfolk coast helps make this a book which, I am sure, will bring much enjoyment.

Aitken Clark, Chief Executive, Broads Authority

Key to tables

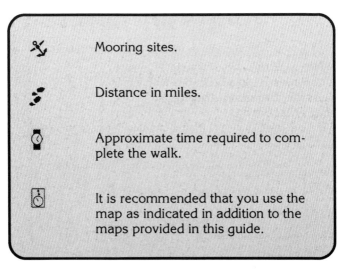

Mooring sites.

Distance in miles.

Approximate time required to complete the walk.

It is recommended that you use the map as indicated in addition to the maps provided in this guide.

Acknowledgements

Debbie Bartlett would like to thank the following for their help with this book:

Graham Kenworthy, railway historian; Martin Warren, Curator of Cromer Museum; Graeme Heyes, of the Norfolk Coast Project; Jill Richards and Declan Keiley of the Broads Authority for advice about Broads footpaths; Sally Whiteford of Norfolk County Council for advice about North Norfolk footpaths.

Special thanks to Jeremy Bryant for advice and support, and to Lucy and Polly whose little legs managed to walk nearly all the way.

Photographic credits

Broads Authority 57, 138
Diana Shipp, Broads Authority 37, 118
Graeme Hayes 20, 21, 128, 131, 132
Jill Richards, Broads Authority 64
National Trust 83, 84
Norfolk County Council Library and Information Service 13, 18, 24, 49, 70, 102, 121, 126
Norfolk Museums Service 90
North Norfolk Railway 129
Richard Denyer 1, This page, 8, 9, 11, 12, 16, 27, 30, 33, 35, 40, 41, 43, 44, 46, 48, 51, 58, 64, 65, 71, 72, 77, 80, 96, 100, 106, 108, 112, 113, 116, 135, 141, 142
Suffolk Wildlife Trust 75
Great Yarmouth Borough Council 87

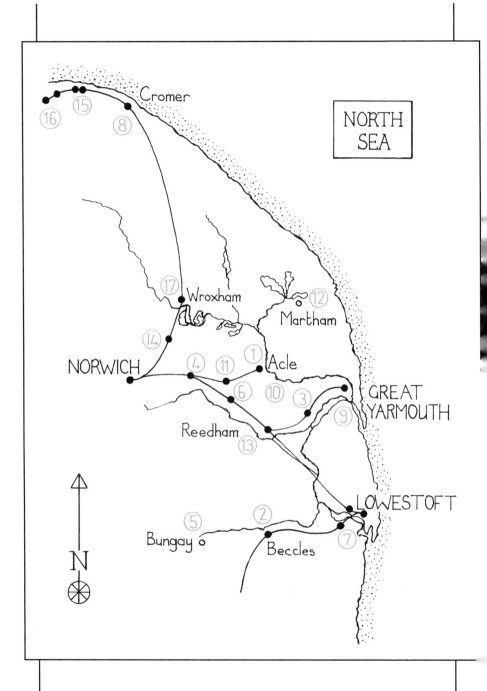

Map showing walk locations

Richard Denyer

RICHARD Denyer's photographs of the Broads reflect his passionate interest in the history, culture and traditions of this unique wetland. He started photographing the area in the early 1980s after studying design and photography at Norwich Art School. His interest lies in capturing the Broads as a living landscape, where people work and pursue patterns of existence that are in harmony with their surroundings. Nowhere is this better illustrated than in Richard's book *Still Waters*, a collection of Broads photographs that is published by Still Waters Press.

> Where moorings are given at the start of the walks they are nearly all free 24-hour Broads Authority moorings. Other moorings may, however, be available close by for which there could be a small charge.

Introduction

WHEN mediaeval man laboured under the soggy task of cutting thousands of squares of peat for fuel, little did he imagine he was helping to shape one of 20th century Britain's most cherished landscapes.

For the Norfolk and Suffolk Broads are largely man-made. The shallow lakes, known as broads, were the result of peat digging over a period of about 300 years for people who had little else in the way of fuel for their fires. Later, in the 14th century the sea level gradually began to rise, and over the centuries the diggings flooded and were abandoned and forgotten. From what must have been unsightly scars on the landscape, there has evolved an invaluable wetland habitat shaped and moulded by the patterns of human existence.

A lone swan pauses at a dyke's edge (R Denyer)

It was not until the 1960s that the true origins of the Broads were discovered. Dr Joyce Lambert, a local scientist, published the findings of her research which were greeted with a degree of incredulity and scepticism. How could these huge broads have been dug by hand by people, without the aid of our sophisticated engineering techniques and machinery of today? The evidence of records was irrefutable, yet even today there are some locals who claim to know better.

Today what makes the Broads special is the variety of habitats and landscape types welded together like a giant jigsaw puzzle. Lose one piece and the overall picture will never be the same again. There is the open water of the broads themselves, the rivers, some slow-winding, others wide with strong tidal currents; the fens with their crops of whispering reeds and sedge which are the thatcher's raw material; the drained marshland, or grazing marsh, where cattle and sheep graze under a huge expansive sky; the carr woodland, and the lively riverside villages with their working boatyards, pubs, shops and homes.

(left) Water, windmills and walking — three central elements of a visit to the Broads

Recreation and the Broads

The abiding attraction of the Broads remains its 200 kilometres of navigable waterway, offering the prospect of unfettered cruising and sailing. The hire boat industry offers people who have never been behind the wheel of a boat before the freedom to take to the water in a safe way without the need for complex instruction.

Yet a visitor 150 years ago to the Broads would have seen a thriving commercial network of rivers and broads populated by black sailed trading wherries carrying every conceivable cargo. The wherries were the lorries of today, and the rivers and broads were the roads and motorways. They linked isolated communities with the rest of Norfolk and were the only feasible commercial carrying route for the ports of Norwich, Lowestoft and Great Yarmouth.

But the arrival of the railways from the mid 19th century onwards proved the death knell of wherry traffic and of the commercial use of the waterways. Instead the Broads was 'discovered' by well-to-do Victorians and Edwardians looking for adventure.

For a time commerce and leisure lived side by side. In winter wherrymen lived their hard life plying their cargoes; in summer some diversified slinging hammocks in the hold, people became the new cargo and the wherryman and his mate became skipper and steward to the holiday party. Wherry builders, ever inventive, saw a new market emerging. Pleasure wherries were built from the 1880s, fitted with cabins, and as Victorian tastes refined, the wherry yacht was developed for customers wanting a sleeker look from the craft. These wherry yachts came with an afterdeck which gave somewhere for parties to lounge gracefully without interfering with the sailing of the craft.

But not everyone wanted to hire such large craft as a wherry, and it was a man named John Loynes who pioneered the hiring of smaller sail boats. Other firms followed his success and in 1908 a landmark was reached when Blakes Norfolk Broads Holidays Ltd was founded to act as an agent for firms, handling their holiday bookings. The firm still thrives today. In the 1920s and the 1930s the motor cruiser emerged on the scene. Now, for the first time, people without any sailing experience could enjoy the Broads. Things were never to be the same again.

The holiday momentum continued after the war, with a gradual shift away from sailing to cruiser holidays. In the 1950s people had paid holiday entitlements, car ownership increased, and more people came to try a holiday with a difference.

An important boat building breakthrough was made in the 1960s with the development of fibreglass hull mouldings. Hire fleets expanded, peaking in the 1970s when there were over 2,500 motor cruisers for hire. Today that number is declining as recessionary pressures bite, but in recent years the number of private boats has increased. In total there are almost 13,000 boats registered for use on the Broads.

Tourism has become a vital, thriving industry of the area, and together with agriculture is one of the mainstays of the local economy. But tourism at times puts severe strain on the Broads. With about a million visitors a year seeing the broads and rivers, this nationally protected area, with its fragile ecology, is under intense recreational pressure. In common with other national parks, and wetlands around the world, the Broads in many ways is being loved to death.

The Broads Authority

Almost 50 years ago, ten areas of England and Wales were singled out as being worthy of special protection as national parks. Despite being recommended, the Broads were not included. It was not until 1978 that a special organisation was set up to look after the Broads. By that time the area had succumbed to severe environmental pressure and the Broads Authority had to put into action a programme of restoration.

In 1989, eleven years after the first Broads Authority was established, an Act of Parliament was passed setting up a new, more powerful authority, with the same status as other national parks. The Broads had finally received the recognition the area deserved, but in the eyes of many it had come 40 years too late. There was a lot of catching up to do.

Today, the main environmental challenges facing the Broads Authority are the restoration of clear water and healthy plant life to the area, a reduction in bank erosion, and restoration of the 2,500 hectares of valuable fens which lie beyond and all around the waterways. Much has already been achieved in the Broads, and a continuing programme of research and experimental management will ensure that steadily and surely this valuable wetland area is restored and enhanced.

Mud-pumping a Broads dyke. A number of broads have had silt removed as an important step towards restoring water quality.

11

Another whisky dear?… Two unlikely deckhands take in some Broads sunshine.

The coming of the railways

Proud men of the Great Eastern. This picture was taken about 1880.

RAILWAYS came late to Norfolk, a county whose people have traditionally looked upon any change with deep suspicion.

The first line was opened in 1844, connecting Great Yarmouth with Norwich. By the turn of the century Norfolk and North Suffolk were crisscrossed with lines; tiny villages had been transformed, communities enlivened by new trade, prosperity and prospects for travelling. In short, the area turned from a declining backwater into a thriving dynamic region.

The fillip which the railways provided was a timely one. The eastern counties of the mid 19th century were impoverished and run down. The textile industry, the mainstay of Norfolk, had all but declined by 1800, and a lack of coal and general dislike of change made industrial development an uphill struggle.

Transport links were poor. Nearly all goods were carried by river — in trading wherries, mainly through the port of Great Yarmouth. This could be slow and until the middle of the 19th century all goods had to be transhipped from sea-going vessels, because none but the smallest of sea-going ships could navigate the shallow waters to the city of Norwich. This meant delays, and the inevitable breakages and pilfering, making river haulage slow and inefficient.

Good roads were practically non-existent. In the early decades of the 19th century only seven per cent of Norfolk's roads were turn-pikes; the remainder were in a sorry condition. It took a four-horse wagon with 24 sacks of grain nearly two days to cover the 50 miles between Norwich and King's Lynn.

If ever a region needed revitalising, it was the eastern counties, and when they did finally arrive, the impact of the railways was instantaneous. In the winter of 1846-7, when the Norwich to London link had finally been made, Norwich merchants sent goods to Ipswich via London — a distance of 196 miles — rather than on 40 miles of road described at the time as being half a yard deep in mud.

Naturally enough the first railway planned for Norfolk was be-tween Norwich and London. In 1834 a prospectus for the Grand Eastern Counties Railway (the 'Grand' was soon dropped) was issued extolling the virtues of railways and highlighting the com-mercial benefits, even going so far as to suggest such an undertak-ing could ease the burden on the poor rates! As the prospectus said:

"...give a new impulse to every branch of industry — furnish directly or indirectly employment for many thousands of hands — and take a large share of the burden of the poor rates on itself; thus multiplying prodigiously the resources of the district, while at the same time it diminished the demands upon them."

Eventually the necessary Parliamentary approval was received for a route from London to Norwich and Great Yarmouth, via Chelmsford, Colchester and Ipswich. It was decided to start work at either end of the line — London to Chelmsford, and Great Yarmouth to Norwich — since these sections seemed to promise the best return. But the London end was beset with financial difficulties, and the whole scheme was ulti-mately scaled down to provide a line only from London to Colchester. Norwich was once again left out in the cold.

A meeting was held in the city to discuss how Norwich could develop its own independent rail link with the capital. A proposal was put forward at this meeting to link Norwich and Great Yar-mouth, and a scheme, formulated by none other than George Stephenson and his son Robert, was supported.

The necessary legal niceties were completed and in April 1843 work got under way, with the resident engineer being Sir Samuel Morton Peto. Robert Stephenson had estimated that the line would cost £7,000 a mile, although in the end it cost £10,000; there were to be no tunnels, no major engineering challenges, and it was a single track of standard gauge.

The official opening of the line was on April 30 1844 when 200 guests, complete with brass band, travelled in the train from Norwich to Great Yarmouth. Once the electric telegraph had given the all-clear, the band struck up with *See the conquering hero comes* and Norfolk's first railway steamed into being. It was quite a day; the train completed the journey in 50 minutes and then there were omnibuses to ferry passengers to the jetty and the beach. Many, we are told, "...availed themselves of this opportunity of enjoying the salubrity of the day and the marine view, while strolling on the sands". The return journey took 44 minutes, and the celebrations were rounded off with nothing short of a banquet in the city.

But amid the euphoria of the opening of the county's first railway, Norfolk had not forgotten its desire for a connection with London. A scheme was put forward to link Norwich with Brandon, (a town near Thetford), which would meet a projected line coming from Newport. This in turn was linked with Bishops Stortford, which had been linked to London since 1842. The Norwich-Brandon section involved the bridging of the River Wensum at Trowse, so a single-track swing bridge, operated by hand, was duly built. In December 1845 the bridge was opened and for the first time it was possible to travel from Great Yarmouth to London (Shoreditch) via Norwich, Brandon, Ely, and Cambridge without changing trains. The 146 miles took about 6 hrs 15 mins.

The Trowse swing bridge lasted until August 1905. By that time it was carrying 170 trains a day which had to crawl over the bridge at 3 mph while picking up a pilot. Not surprisingly it was an intolerable bottleneck so was replaced by a new, power operated, double-track bridge. This in turn survived until February 1987 when the present bridge, single-track, but with modern operating procedures was built.

During the next few dramatic years of the mid 19th century many more lines were added to the eastern region network, bringing West Norfolk into the system with lines connecting King's Lynn, March, Wisbech, Swaffham, Dereham and Fakenham. South Norfolk also became well served with stations at such tiny villages as Tivetshall. Beccles and Bungay too gained railway status.

Lowestoft and Great Yarmouth

A visionary man named Sir Samuel Morton Peto has been called the maker of Lowestoft. It was he who was the driving force behind the construction of the new Lowestoft Harbour, which, closely linked with railway expansion, turned the sleepy Suffolk coastal fishing village into a thriving port.

The 11^1/$_2$-mile Reedham to Lowestoft branch opened to passengers in 1847 with Sir Samuel as chairman and principal shareholder. The Lowestoft Railway and Harbour Company had already provided Lowestoft with a harbour boasting 3,000 feet of wharf frontage, powered cranes, a bucket dredging machine, fishing facilities and a pier with double-track tramway and turntable at each end. The company was taken over in 1848 by Eastern Counties Railways who set out to make Lowestoft a major port. Despite internal wranglings the venture was by and large successful. In 1845 the number of vessels docking at Lowestoft was 410, and by 1851 it was 1636. Grain, livestock, butter, meat and dairy products came in from Europe.

Great Yarmouth

In 1851 Great Yarmouth was described as squalid and over-crowded. The arrival of the railways in Norfolk had not had the expected effect on the port, which had suffered in the face of new investment at Lowestoft. But the potential remained, mainly from the fishing industry, and from the burgeoning holiday trade. Private investment in the herring trade by 1892 amounted to about £500,000 and by the turn of the century hundreds of thousands of fish were being transported by rail to London, Manchester, Birmingham and other urban centres.

But the railways' major contribution to the development of Great Yarmouth was in the holiday industry. The Eastern and Midland

Railway (later part of the Midland and Great Northern Joint System) brought trade from the Midlands and the North. Great Yarmouth was to become one of the best served resorts of its size in the country. By 1904 there was a non-stop run from London to Great Yarmouth of just 150 minutes. The schedules were lost during the First World War, but quickly

Railway across the marshes. A Regional Railways train trundles towards Acle from Great Yarmouth.

reintroduced after hostilities ended, although by 1939 the time had increased to 155 minutes and the service ran only on Saturdays.

The Saturday holiday specials continue to this day at Great Yarmouth. During the week small cross-country trains, usually with two coaches, trundle across the marshes. But on a Saturday in August, holiday trains packed with excited children and weary parents arrive at Great Yarmouth; and make ready to return to Norwich packed with tired children and even more weary parents making their way home.

Cromer and Sheringham

The Cromer of the 1860s was a genteel resort, frequented by those who sought refuge from the curse of the excursionist and the day trippers who flocked to Great Yarmouth. It was a place of peace and tranquility, so when a railway company was formed in 1865 to build a line from Norwich to North Walsham, a shiver ran down the spine of Cromer's elite. The Great Eastern Railway could not contemplate the prospect of building lines to isolated patches of population such as were found east of Norwich, but did offer a form of sponsorship to any independent company which took up the challenge. The East Norfolk company accepted that challenge and planned to build from Whitlingham Junction to North Walsham, with the Great Eastern Railway actually working the line in return for 50 per cent of the receipts.

Work began in 1865, but money was short and when the contractor died it stopped altogether. Work resumed in 1870 with a new contractor, but money and time were still short so an extension had to be sought. This was coupled with permission to extend the line to Cromer, making the scheme a more viable investment since North Walsham was but a small market town. In 1874 North Walsham was reached, with Gunton in 1876 and finally Cromer in 1877.

By 1883 there were seven daily trains from Norwich (1s 6d return (7½p) or 1s (5p) after noon), but connections were poor and the railway seems to have had little impact in its early years. But a new threat to those seeking peace and quiet at Cromer was soon to come from another direction. In June 1887 the Eastern and Midlands Railway completed its line from Melton Constable (the Crewe of Norfolk) to link up with Holt, Sheringham and Cromer. The significance of this was that it provided a link between the Midlands and a ready market of holidaymakers and day trippers eager to discover the North Norfolk coast.

The competition from this new line encouraged more efficient services via Norwich. In 1897 there started a non-stop daily, summer only, Cromer Express to and from London taking just 175 minutes. In 1899 a three-car restaurant was attached and in 1907 the train was given a twelve-coach corridor set and renamed the Norfolk Coast Express. Until its end in 1914, it was the pride of the Great Eastern Railway.

One problem to be overcome was that the section from North Walsham to Cromer was single-track. With an increase in traffic this became cumbersome and inefficient to operate, so a system was installed called the Tyers Electric Tablet System which allowed the safe passage of trains between passing loops. Very basically it meant there was one metal 'key' or tablet for a stretch of single track line which had to be passed from train to train to ensure that only one train at a time used a particular section of track. Improvements to the process were made in 1906 with the introduction of a system which meant trains could exchange tablets at a higher speed. The system still survives on parts of the Norwich to Sheringham line today.

Wroxham, on the line from Whitlingham Junction to North Walsham, developed as the railway centre for the Broads. From the 1880s water-bound visitors had arrived at Wroxham to pick up their boats and cruise through the miles of inland waterways, and by 1965 over 30,000 tickets were collected in Wroxham.

The proliferation of lines in North Norfolk was short-lived. Despite the Beeching cuts, the Melton Constable to Cromer branch line survived for the sake of the scattered villages which relied on the railway for transport. But by 1964 closure could no longer be averted and the line from the railway village of Melton Constable to Sheringham was closed.

Melton Constable junction East, taken in 1927. This tiny Norfolk village was once called the 'Crewe of Norfolk'.

The story of the railways and Norfolk is one of speed and transformation. In little more than a century a network of parallel lines had been instrumental in shaping the economic and social pattern of the county. Long-distance drovers had been put out of business, some towns and villages doomed to stagnation, while others were enlivened by mass tourism and commerce. But perhaps even more significant was the increased mobility and choice the railways gave to Norfolk people, ending, for better or worse, the isolation of the county.

Recently the railways have enjoyed something of a revival. City dwellers weary of the smog and pressures of London life have sought refuge in the Norfolk and Suffolk countryside. Electrification of the the Norwich–Liverpool Street line in 1987 meant it was feasible to commute on a daily basis. One early morning train was nicknamed the 'Filofax Flyer' in recognition of the commuters who used it. But this revival too had its disadvantages. House prices in Norfolk and Suffolk rocketed, putting them way beyond the reach of the average local buyer.

And what of the cross country lines? Regional Railways struggles with a lack of investment and outdated rolling stock. It has been said that a Victorian signalman would still feel at home in many of the county's aging signal boxes where coal still arrives by the bucket to feed the pot-bellied stove which is the hub of the signal-man's workplace. On many lines there are still sections where paraffin lamps on signals are still in use, and a railwayman has to keep them topped up with paraffin regularly.

There remains the continual fear of closure of some of the rural lines. In 1983 the closure of the Norwich–Great Yarmouth line, via Reedham, became imminent and the date was given as October 29 1985 but a combined effort by user groups and local authorities undertook to provide an annual £52,500 to help maintain the track. In the '90s, with privatisation looming, there is an undercurrent of uncertainty, although more up-to-date rolling stock and signalling is being introduced to replace the bone-shakers which, in railway jargon, are 'life-expired'.

For a region which takes in the Broads, a national park, and a coastal stretch of great beauty, the railways are as significant today as they were 120 years ago, although for different reasons. Today about a million visitors a year come to the Broads, and most come in cars. They pollute the air, they clog up the roads, and they park in all the wrong places. The trains offer visitors the chance to walk and experience the countryside without adding to its already im-mense problems. A Dutch national park has adopted a slogan: 'Your car can live without you for one day.' Food for thought when you are sitting in yet another traffic jam.

The fishing tradition

CROMER and Sheringham, like much of the North Norfolk coast, are established on soft glacial sands and muds. During the last ice age a massive sheet of ice, hundreds of metres thick, swept down from the north like a gigantic bulldozer, pushing before it a mighty pile of debris. Today the remains of this debris forms the Cromer Ridge, which is five miles wide and stretches for 20 miles.

Fishing has been a way of life for generations of North Norfolk families

Cromer Ridge once stretched several miles further out to sea, but over the centuries it has fallen prey to the relentless pounding of the North Sea, which continues unabated today. Where land is undefended it is lost at a rate of a metre a year.

In many ways Cromer, Sheringham and other North Norfolk coastal towns have endured, down the centuries, a love-hate relationship with the sea. Prosperous ports have been swallowed up by the waves, forcing people to retreat further inland. Yet the sea has brought great prosperity, yielding a rich harvest for fishermen and sea-faring traders.

The most famous of these ports to succumb to the sea's relentless undermining was Shipden, established a little north of the Cromer we know today. It disappeared over the cliffs in the late 14th century and all that remain are pieces of flint masonry, several hundred metres out to sea from the pier, which could once be seen at very low tide. Known as Church Rock, it is the remains of the church of St Peter, Shipden. Legend would have us believe that the bells of this sunken church toll in times of stormy weather.

The people of Shipden realised their town was to be lost, and in about 1400 started building a new church which we know today as Cromer church. It is a grand structure even by Norfolk church standards and has the highest tower in Norfolk, an indication of the wealth of the town in mediaeval times.

Over a century later, Sheringham was continuing its own battle with the invading sea. In the 1580s the town attempted to build itself a harbour to give the fishing industry some sort of protection and haven. The project proved too ambitious and ended amid allegations of corruption, as the silt built up around the piers of the harbour, but not before some £2,000 had been spent.

The wealth of these towns was founded on the fishing industry and on other trade. Demand for fish was much higher than today. Before Henry VIII broke with Rome in the early 16th century and England was a Catholic country, fish was an important part of the diet and had to be eaten every Friday and on numerous saints' days. Herring, mackerel, cod, and

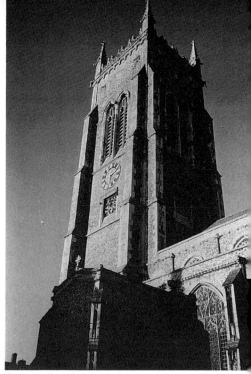

Cromer church, a towering monument to God, and to the wealth of the mediaeval wool trade

ling, as well as lobsters and crabs were caught according to season. Other trade consisted mainly of importing coal and exporting corn, and coal ships could be seen off the Cromer coast as recently as the 1870s. It was the coming of the railways which finally killed off this trade.

The Great Boats

The second part of the 19th century saw the emergence of 'The Great Boats'. These were essentially luggers which allowed the sea-faring men to carry out long-shore, or deep-sea fishing, remaining at sea for long periods to fish for whatever was in season. The year began in spring when there was crabbing off the Yorkshire coast and later off the Cromer coast. Smaller crab boats would some-times be strapped to the luggers for this task. In autumn, herring or mackerel were the main catch and in winter attention was turned to cod, working again from the Yorkshire ports.

These luggers could not land at Cromer or Sheringham. Instead catches and supplies had to be ferried to and from the beach. Perhaps for this reason the boats only returned two or three times a year. The fleet was at its peak in the 1860s when there were about 40 luggers, but by 1890 it had shrunk to a dozen as the steam drifter took over.

Crabs and Shannocks

By the end of the 19th century the heyday of the Great Boats, or luggers, was over, but there was still plenty to fill the nets and pots of the 'Crabs' of Cromer and the 'Shannocks' of Sheringham. Shellfish, mainly crabs and lobsters, had always been an important element of the fisheries, but when the long-shore fishing declined, the shellfish became the mainstay of the local fishing economy, although fishermen continued to fish for whatever catch was in season.

An important development in the crabbing industry had been the introduction of the crab pot in the 1860s which was to revolutionise the crab-catching business, making it much quicker and more efficient. Pots were baited with flat fish and worked on the same principle as an old fashioned mouse trap. About 20 to 25 crab pots were roped together to form a 'shank' which were set out over about one third of a mile of sea bed. Most boats then worked as many as eight shanks, emptying the pots early each day and sending the crabs to market. The most common vessel was the crab boat, a clinker-built double-ended boat, fitted with a lug-sail and later with an engine. The sailing crab boats were small enough to be landed on the shore and carried up and down the beach on their oars. Modern boats are heavier and must be launched with tractors and trailers.

The crab pots proved so efficient that stocks came under pressure and this led to an inquiry into the fisheries of Norfolk, one conclusion of which was that crab and lobster fishing had become impoverished to an alarming degree. "If some remedy is not speedily applied, their extinction is feared," the inquiry reported.

The remedy was an Act of Parliament in 1876 which limited the size of crabs to be caught to four-and-a-quarter inches, and the size of lobsters to 7ins, later amended to 8ins. Peak years for the crabbing industry of North Norfolk were around the turn of the century. Around 1875 there were an estimated 200 boats working 4,000 pots; in 1909 there were 109 boats with a total of 8,000 pots; in 1924 there were 65 boats and 7,200 pots.

The decline in the number of boats is undoubtedly linked to social changes at the turn of the century. Cromer and Sheringham were becoming popular with day trippers. Hotels and boarding houses were being built, and the growing building trade offered fishermen a reliable all-year-round income. Those who continued fishing would diversify in the summer, hiring out bathing machines, swimming costumes, towels, deck-chairs and goat-carts for rides across the sands. The fishermen were all part of the attraction, and to this day, watching the catches come ashore is a source of fascination for many visitors.

The most telling change in recent memory however, has been the introduction of hydraulic winches or pot-haulers fitted to boats which allow the crab pots to be mechanically pulled in, a task formerly done by hand. The first pot-hauler was fitted in 1967 and their use was soon widespread, allowing each boat to work more pots. The effects of this modernisation were far-reaching as the fishing became concentrated in the hands of a few larger boats.

Fishing communities are always tightly knit, and the North Norfolk fishermen were, and are, no exception. They have always been fiercely independent and justly proud of their fishing skills, their seamanship and their hardiness. But the women, left behind while their menfolk went to sea, should not be forgotten. Theirs were the long hours at home, drying endless baskets of soaking fishing gear, bringing up families in tiny fishermen's cottages, helping to prepare bait, lines and dressing and selling crabs. But worst of all, waiting, waiting for their menfolk to return from a hostile sea which will always claim its victims.

Fishermen have always made up the crews of the lifeboats of Cromer and until recently, Sheringham. At the sound of the maroon the crews would drop everything and run for the boats, very often after long hours at sea themselves. Cromer's first lifeboat was founded in 1804, followed in Sheringham in 1838, those early boats being powered by oars alone. Fathers and sons have manned the boats for generations, and time and time again their bravery in launching to save fellow seamen has been put to the sternest test. Perhaps the most famous lifeboatman of all was Henry Blogg of Cromer, the most decorated lifeboatman ever, and a national hero.

Today only a handful of fishing boats work out of Cromer and Sheringham. In recent years the six or so boats at Sheringham have had a hard time because the physical changes to the beach have made it too steep to land their boats. At Cromer about a dozen boats continue to fish in the crabbing season, but the pattern of fishing life has changed.

Sons are less likely to follow their fathers into fishing. Many fishermen also turn their hands to different trades such as building and will drift back into fishing when the season is right. And there has also been the emergence of the so-called 'after tea' fisherman who puts to sea after a day's work elsewhere.

Few, if any, have made their fortune fishing and today it remains a precarious business. As recently as 1993 four Sheringham boats were damaged when gales and storms lashed the North Norfolk coast, washing away £10,000 of investment. Fishing may have embraced many modern techniques, but it still remains at the beck and call of the unpredictable sea.

The Poppyland legend

Victorian gentility at play on Sheringham West Beach. This was taken between 1891 and 1894.

The two four-horsed coaches which ply daily between Norwich and Cromer do not convey the shoals of noisy excursionists which overflow Yarmouth and Lowestoft. In the months of August and September Cromer is full of the better class of seaside visitors. In those months it is as nearly perfect as a watering place may be.
G Christopher Davies, circa 1873.

UNTIL the railway opened in 1877, Cromer was a select watering hole, patronised mainly by the gentility while Sheringham remained largely undiscovered. The railway put Cromer and the North Norfolk coast within easy reach of many more day trippers, and the town soon responded with the opening of hotels and boarding houses, ready to cater for every whim of the visitors' needs.

But on one telling occasion, Cromer could not find a bed for one of its visitors. Clement Scott was an influential London drama critic who came to the town in the 1880s collecting material for an article he was writing for the Daily Telegraph. Having observed the holidaymakers at play, he tried to find somewhere to stay, but could not find a bed for love or money. Instead Scott headed along the coast towards Overstrand and turned inland attracted by a ruined church tower.

As he reported, he found "a blue sky without a cloud across it; a sea sparkling under a haze of heat; wild flowers in profusion around me, poppies predominating everywhere". Scott found lodgings at Mill House where he met the miller's daughter, Louie Jermy, and it was to here he was to return many times, bringing friends to enjoy his discovery. The Poppyland legend was born.

A poem he wrote, 'The Garden of Sleep', about the ruined church tower and its graveyard, was at the centre of the legend:

'Neath the blue of the sky, in the green of the corn,
It is there that the royal red poppies are born!
Brief days of desire, and long dreams of delight
They are mine when my Poppy-Land cometh in sight.

The poem was published, widely-read, set to music, and was to appear on many postcards and other publications about Scott and Poppyland. His writings about Poppyland made the area desperately fashionable. His theatrical and artistic connections brought some colourful characters to visit, as well as a few wealthy ones, and the village of Overstrand later became known as the 'The Village of Millionaires'. Poppyland also became an industry. The coast from Mundesley to Sheringham was marketed as being part of the Poppyland legend, promoted as a picturesque and desirable holiday spot.

The Great Eastern Railway took up the theme and produced posters encouraging people to visit North Norfolk. With the legend came the souvenirs; bright poppies blossomed on thousands of postcards, on china everything from candle holders to full tea services — these have now become collectors items. A Cromer chemist, Daniel Davison, produced what was to become one of the most famous souvenirs, a perfume called Poppyland Bouquet. It was sold worldwide and made until 1930.

Poppyland was to popularise the North Norfolk coast, and even further afield to such an extent that Scott was later to lament the change. He wrote: "The Cromer that we visit now is not the Cromer I wrote about but a few short years ago as my beloved Poppyland."

The Garden of Sleep at the centre of Poppyland succumbed to the effects of crumbling cliffs in 1916 when the tower without a church, which was featured in Scott's writings, toppled to the beach, the garden slipping away with it. But the Poppyland legend lived on for a while, and more recently has seen a revival of interest.

The holiday trade today remains the principal industry of Cromer and Sheringham, with people staying in hotels, guest houses, flats, caravans and tents. The poppies still bloom in the fields, where their seeds can lie dormant for many years below the ground.

Caring for Norfolk's coast

The beauty of the Norfolk coast today hinges on a combination of elements, from the remote coastline, rolling farmland, tranquil river valleys and quiet villages, all contained under a mighty sky, and bordered by the unmistakable presence of the sea.

In 1968, 451 square kilometres of the Norfolk coast, including the stretch from Snettisham to Mundesley, was designated as an Area of Outstanding Natural Beauty. Since then the coast has become subject to increasing pressures, particularly from visitors, who have the potential to spoil what they come to enjoy.

In 1992 the Norfolk Coast Project was set up to ensure that the use of the area does not destroy its natural beauty. It is a partnership between individuals, local authorities, statutory agencies, conservation organisations, industry and others with an interest in the area. Its objectives are to conserve and enhance the natural beauty of the area, improve public enjoyment and understanding, and to promote sustainable social and economic development. One new initiative is the Sunday Explorer Bus which operates during the summer connecting Norwich and other county towns and villages with the North Norfolk coast. The bus is a joint venture with Norfolk County Council and aims to ease traffic congestion on the coast and give people without cars the chance to enjoy this beautiful part of the county.

Acle to South Walsham

Acle is a village in the heart of the Broads, and this walk takes in some of the glorious landscapes which are so characteristic of the area, including a magical nature reserve, and a sweeping riverbank walk with views across open marshland.

Start	Acle Railway Bridge
Finish	Acle Railway Station
⚓	Free Broads Authority Moorings at Fleet Dyke near South Walsham Broad
👣	12 miles
⌚	4½ hours
🗺	Landranger sheet 134

Cruisers jostle for position at Acle Bridge on the River Bure

THURSDAY is market day at Acle, traditionally a day when the village comes alive. Permission was granted for the market way back in the 13th century. In its heyday it was a massive affair with farmers driving their cattle over the Reedham Ferry to attend the auction. In a later era, the cattle were then driven from the sale yard to the station where they were held in cattle pens before being loaded in wagons. The noise of the beasts braying was ear-splitting.

The cattle trains stopped in the early 1960s and lorries took over. Sadly, today, Acle market has no livestock. Even sales of chickens and rabbits have been stopped because of new regulations about cage sizes. But the bicycle auction is renowned for its bargains, and dead stock throws up everything from beehives to bidets. The tearoom does a wonderful cuppa, out of a thick white china mug, and wickedly sugary doughnuts.

Starting from the Norwich platform, turn your back on the platform, and then turn right out of the station down a narrow footpath. (If travelling from Great Yarmouth, then cross the foot-bridge first.) When this path joins the road, turn left, walking under the underpass. At the junction with the main village street, bear right, opposite the pretty round-towered thatched church of St Edmund's, and continue through the village.

The street bends sharply right, but our route is straight on, keeping the village sign to the right, and the small supermarket on the left, until reaching a cross-roads. Go straight across up a small lane called Pyebush Lane. The playing field comes into view on the right and the land turns to a track as it bends left past the cemetery and towards open fields.

A narrow path now, it leads between two fields with a view down and to the right towards the Bure. The tiny church of Fishley St Mary stands isolated on a slight rise. This beautiful church was once at the heart of the village of Fishley, but no-one has ever really got to the bottom of how or why the community dwindled. Today the church still has no electricity but manages to power three electric lights by using a generator.

The path crosses a road and then continues in a straight line through the next field, bending left through a hedge-lined corridor and emerging in the village of Upton. Turn left, and then at the crossroads near the village shop, turn right. Follow the road through the village and then as it bends sharply to the left.

Leaving the cultivated gardens, the hanging baskets and the mix of tumbledown farm buildings and smart new executive dwellings behind, the countryside opens out. To the right are The Doles, an area of woodland, in which is hidden Upton Broad, an isolated Broad, cut off from the river, and a glorious nature reserve.

The route then leaves the country roads and turns off right along a public footpath, waymarked with a Broads Authority green arrow. Track turns to grassy path, and heads towards the woods, at first skirting the edge and then plunging into the trees. The path then leaves the shelter of woodland, still following the line of the trees, but with open fields to the left. It passes through a small area of reeds, turning left over a wooden plank bridge where huge dragon-flies are wont to bask in the summer heat.

The next section is a magical stretch, the path dipping in and out of the wood, at one point going along a boardwalk because the ground is so lush and damp. If you walk this way in summer then be sure not to miss the wild raspberries.

The path leaves the woods for the last time and continues to-wards a set of farm buildings. Go into the farmyard and turn right following the waymark arrow. This leads to a junction, turn right, again following the waymark arrow. A further 100 metres on the right is Upton Fen Nature Reserve, owned and managed by the Norfolk Naturalists' Trust. It is made up of 50 acres of fen, woodland and dykes, and is part of a larger Site of Special Scientific Interest, an indication of the value of the area. It is spring-fed which means the water quality is high, giving many rare plants and insects the chance to thrive.

A network of footpaths goes round the reserve and it is possible to see the fruits of the Trust's labours. It is worth making a detour if you have time.

Continue on the road, which bends to the left, and then take the waymarked footpath on the right, cutting across the field following the line of a hedge. This is slightly raised and there is a magnificent view to the right towards the River Bure and the ruins of St Benet's Abbey, a view enlivened by the presence of gleaming white sails.

The path crosses into the adjacent field, keeping the hedge on the right, and comes out on a road. Turn right, and then bear right at the junction to take you past South Walsham Broad on the left. Here there is a tiny parish staithe from where you can enjoy the activity of the Broad.

South Walsham Broad has something of a colourful history. The Broad is actually divided into two — the inner broad and the outer broad. It is possible to moor on the outer broad, while the inner remains a more tranquil haven, although being surrounded with trees it is not an ideal place for sailing. This situation arose when at the turn of the century the question of public access to the broad was challenged. The owner of the time had put up posts and wire across the stretch of water dividing the inner and the outer broads, which had enraged locals. The owner added fuel to the fire by mooring his houseboat, *The Ark*, near the entrance. As the paper of the day reported, from a distance it appeared to be armed with guns and "men of formidable appearance". In fact all he had was a hand-operated fire engine and what villagers mistook for a machine gun was merely the barrel of an old telescope.

It was somehow all resolved peaceably, and the right of way to the inner broad restored, although no swimming, mooring, or fishing was allowed, and that situation remains to this day.

The route continues along the road, the broad unfortunately hidden by buildings, passing a shop on the left, houses, and a small mooring basin, until turning into a path leading to the head of Fleet Dyke. The dyke was cut to connect the broad with the river Bure. The walking along Fleet Dyke is at first enclosed with woods on the other side of the dyke. But it eventually opens out giving a view to the left over Ranworth Flood, an area of reed beds which are still annually cut for thatching. Ranworth church, known as the Cathedral of the Broads, can also be seen, while straight ahead lies St Benet's Abbey.

When the dyke joins the river Bure the Abbey ruins stand directly opposite. So near, but yet so far. Unfortunately unless you can hitch a lift across the river it is not possible to get closer.

ℹ *St Benet's Abbey is thought to have been founded in AD1020 on land granted by King Canute to a religious group already occupying the site. Over the next hundred years it was endowed with many gifts of land, bringing in a healthy income. By the end of the 13th century St Benet's owned property in 76 Norfolk parishes. One of its most famous benefactors was Sir John Fastolf of Caister Castle — the Falstaff of Shakespeare's plays. He and his wife were buried in the chapel that he built on the site.*

St Benet's was in fact the only religious house in England to escape the zeal of Henry VIII when he dissolved the monasteries. It was laid down in 1536 that the Bishop of Norwich should take on the abbacy of St Benet's, and that 12 monks should be kept there for the keeping of divine services. But the last monk left in 1545; the land was let out to farm, and the buildings became a convenient source of stone. Material from the abbey has been found as far away as the Duke of Norfolk's palace in Norwich. The present brick mill over the gate was built late in the 18th century, mainly for drainage. Its top and sails were blown off in a gale in 1863.

But the spirit of St Benet's lives on. In 1987 a new landmark was erected, a cross of English oak from the Royal Estate at Sandringham, marking the high altar where daily the monks would have gathered to celebrate Eucharist. On the first Sunday in August the Bishop of Norwich sails to St Benet's on board a wherry to conduct an open air service, accompanied by a flotilla of craft. Once again, hymns and prayers rise up from the sacred ground.

The river along this stretch is wide and is popular sailing and cruising ground. Thurne church can be seen ahead, as the Bure is rapidly nearing the meeting point with the River Thurne. At the wide confluence, there is a heaven-sent bench from which you can enjoy the spectacle of dinghies, yachts, cruisers and day-boats all jostling for position on the rivers.

Hymns and prayers from the sacred ground of St Benet's Abbey.

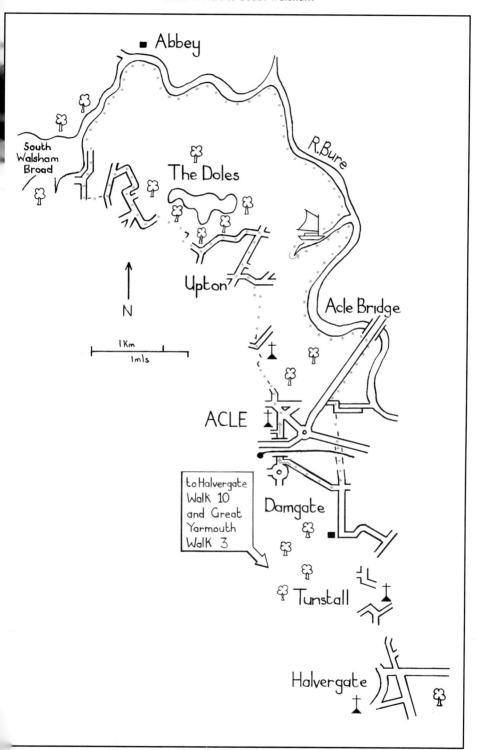

The path continues to follow the riverbank, with the vast expanse of Upton and South Walsham marshes to the right and the hue and cry from the river on the left. From the marshes you may hear the plaintive call of the redshank or the ringing cry of the oystercatcher as they nest among the grazing cattle. In winter they are joined by large flocks of golden plover.

The next dyke which joins the river is Upton Dyke. At its head is Whelpton's boatyard, with a hire fleet consisting only of sailing craft. Also in dry dock at Upton is another classic sailing craft, the trading wherry *Maud*. She is owned by Linda and Vincent Pargeter, a couple from Essex, whose painstaking restoration, lasting perhaps ten years, will eventually see *Maud* afloat once more. From her temporary resting place at Upton it is possible to gain a clearer

Linda and Vincent Pargeter, proud owners of the trading wherry Maud, *which is undergoing restoration*

picture of the construction of a wherry. Linda and Vincent have become quite used to a stream of curious visitors who poke their heads under the awning.

It all began in 1981 when *Maud* was floated from the mud at Ranworth Broad near the Norfolk Naturalists' Trust floating conservation centre where she had been sunk. The Pargeters were given the wherry by the Norfolk Naturalists' Trust on the understanding that she would be restored. Under the full glare of regional television cameras two 25-ton cranes eased *Maud* into position at Upton Dyke. Restoration has been undertaken with grant aid from the Broads Authority and is a marathon project. But what a sensation it will be when *Maud* takes to her native waters again.

Continue the walk up the other side of dyke and carry on along the riverbank. The path meanders with the river all the way to Acle Bridge from where people say you could once count over 20 windpumps.

Cross the road and turn right, following the specially-constructed footpath running alongside the busy road. This ends close to a pub. Turn left at the pub down a track leading to Acle Dyke. At the head of the dyke turn right towards the fields, following the signpost for Weavers' Way. This route takes you between fields, with open views to the left. Here on a clear day you can see Great Yarmouth. Cross the main road, taking care because cars seem incapable of driving slowly along this stretch. It is known both as the Acle Straight and as Acle New Road, even though it was completed by the Acle Turnpike Trust in 1831 and included a link road joining up with the

Three wherries in glorious harmony on the Broads.

village of Halvergate. To have built such a road across boggy terrain was no mean feat of engineering and it contributed substantially to the economic development of Acle since it cut the trip to Yarmouth by three miles five furlongs.

The path, still Weavers' Way, continues between fields where cattle and sheep graze, crossing the railway line, until a crossroad of tracks is reached. Weavers' Way continues straight ahead, but our route lies to the right. This passes the sewage works, not often a landmark but in this case it is the site of an interesting experiment by Anglian Water Services.

In the mid 1980s at Acle Sewage Works, a bed of reeds was planted on an area 100 metres by 35 metres with a 1 in 20 slope towards the middle. The idea was to filter sewage onto the reed bed, allowing the natural chemical process to break down and "treat" the sewage. It was not a new idea, but Acle was targeted as having the right level of population (about 2,800, producing a flow of 500 cubic metres a day) and was felt to be an appropriate site since it was situated in the heart of the Broads.

Half the flow was to be treated by the natural method, half by conventional means at the sewage plant which already existed. The experiment was successful, but it was soon realised Acle's growing population was putting added demand on the sewage plant and a much bigger area of reed bed would be needed. In the event it was decided to use the reed bed as a 'polisher', as a final cleansing process in the sewage treatment. During the experiment the reed (which originated from nearby Cantley) has flourished and now grows to a height of nine or ten feet. The engineer in charge says he has never had to carry out a day's maintenance on the plants and it has brought an added bonus: wildlife is not usually associated with sewage treatment plants, but Acle is an exception. Visit the sewage plant at twilight and you will be rewarded with the uplifting sound of birdsong.

The track turns to a road, past a small industrial estate on the right and thence past houses. This is Damgate, once a separate community with its own pub and shop. The track joins another road, turn right and take the path on the left, just before the railway bridge, signposted to the station.

Beccles and Geldeston

Beccles Tower is a landmark for miles around. It dominates the skyline on this walk to the picture-postcard village of Geldeston and back to Beccles along the River Waveney's edge. Yet this magnificent tower was sold for just one penny, but it was not the bargain it may have seemed! A shorter route round Beccles Marshes is also described. This could be done separately.

Start	Beccles Railway Station
Finish	Beccles Railway Station
⚓	Free 24-hour Broads Authority moorings at Geldeston Lock or Beccles bypass bridge
👣	11 miles
⌚	4 hours
🗺	Landranger sheet 134

Beccles church tower

Boating and fishing on the Waveney; good rowing boats at fourpence per hour; sailing yachts at proportionate prices, according to size; good roads for cycling; old-world scenery for photographers and artists. What more can one desire?

SO mused a visitor to Beccles in the 1880s when the picturesque town on the Waveney was becoming established as a holiday resort. It seems hard to imagine today, looking at the fine Georgian architecture, manicured lawns and smart boats, that Beccles was once a thriving, bustling port.

Leaving the station behind you, walk straight across the mini-roundabout up Station Road. Cross straight over the set of traffic lights and continue a little further until you emerge in the Market Street. To the right is St Michael's Church, surely one of the most unusual in the Broads in that its 97-foot high bell-tower is separate from the main body of the church.

The tower is like a beacon, rising up from the town and visible for miles. A plaque on one of its walls records an unusual transaction: "With this Beccles Penny of 1795 the sixteenth century Tower was bought for Beccles in 1972". A beautiful tower for just a

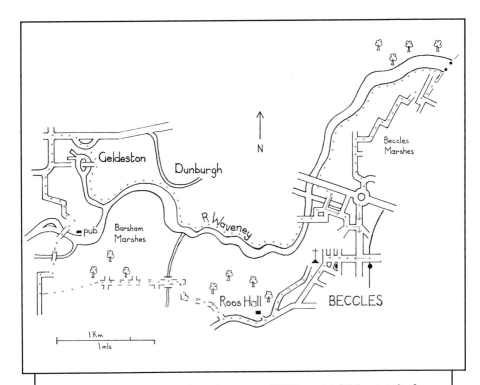

penny? There was a catch — between 1973 and 1977 a total of £68,000 was raised to restore the outside.

It was probably built away from the main body of the church for engineering reasons. Old church documents state: "Not safe to build the steeple on the cliffside", which suggests why it was not built at the usual west end of the church.

The church itself was built between 1350 and 1400 by the Abbott of Bury St Edmunds, but work on the tower did not start until around 1500 and took about forty years to complete. The diary of a bell-ringer records how the bells were rung in October 1798 when Nelson 'took nine ships of the line' and in December 1805, on Thanksgiving Day, for the victory gained by Lord Nelson. Horatio Nelson's parents were married in Beccles church.

Continue from Market Street into New Market, the church and tower still to the right. Beccles is unusual in having two market places — and the area known as New Market was actually in use as early as the 13th century. Our way lies left into Ballygate. Beccles is awash with gates — Northgate, Blyburgate, Sheepgate, and Saltgate — all once routes out of the old town. Despite two serious fires in Beccles in the 16th and 17th centuries much of its historic architecture still remains, and the layout of the town is still reminiscent of a mediaeval town with narrow streets, winding lanes and connecting alleyways.

The houses in Ballygate, like so many in Beccles, are an architectural delight. Their solid form and symmetry confers an air of

Unloading sedge in the summer sun

respectability and dependability on the town. Just past a round tower-like building with a wherry weather vane there is a fine view across marshes towards the river. A steep footpath forks off the pavement, and steps take you down to a lower road. Turn left, walking past the recreation field on the right, and an informal park on the left, until the road curls towards the left to join the main road. Turn right, heading out of Beccles, passing Roos Hall on the right, with its decorative chimneys, and past the sign that announces the parish of Barsham has officially begun.

Look out for a house on a hill on the left. Just beyond this on the right side of the road is another house with a track forking off right passing in front of it. Take this track, leaving the bustle of Beccles behind and the roar of the traffic on the main road. It leads through open farmland, between arable land and grazing meadows. The route is waymarked with Angles Way signs, a 77-mile long distance footpath from Great Yarmouth to Knettishall Heath Country Park near Thetford. The round tower of Barsham church will come into view on the left, (the author Adrian Bell is buried here). There is then a farm building to the right, and a little further on just past a house on the left there is a junction in the track.

Barsham is to the left, the farm is to the right, but our way lies straight across along a grassy track at the edge of a field. (The Angles Way sign is posted on the telegraph pole.) Duck under the power lines and at the end of the field go straight into the next field. The path cuts off the corner of this field heading towards a stile. Cross this stile, and a little further on, cross the next stile which takes you into the adjacent field, following the line of the fence up a slight hill.

At the top of the rise, you reap the reward for what has perhaps not been the most memorable of country slogs. The view looking down on the Waveney Valley is stunning, the river meandering gently through the soft marsh. For many, there is little to equal the unspoilt wildness of the Waveney Valley, and viewed from up here, it is hard to disagree.

The field slopes down again and at the end there is another stile. Cross this and turn right down the lane. Ignore the next public footpath signpost and Angles Way sign which is to the left, and continue on the lane as it curls round to the right, through a complex of pumping houses, until the track turns to grass. A Broads Authority waymarked route and stile points you left across the field towards the river.

There is something especially lush and fertile about this area of marsh. The grass is greener and the swans which graze in graceful pairs seem whiter than white. As you plod across the field a certain hush seems to descend, as if somehow this section of beautiful valley has remained undiscovered. To complete the fairytale you cross a wooden bridge over a dyke before crossing a larger metalwork bridge which marks the end of tidal navigation on the Waveney. Another two bridges over dykes and streams take you into the grounds of Geldeston Locks pub, where a well-earned pint is likely to be in order.

Geldeston, or Shipmeadow Lock, was in use up until 1934, one of three locks enabling wherries to pass the four miles to Bungay. The last owners of this stretch of navigation from Geldeston to Bungay were W D and A E Walker, who were Bungay merchants. Earlier it had been in the ownership of Matthias Kerrison, a man who made his fortune during the Napoleonic War and was said to have died a millionaire in 1827. It is not clear when the lock was first installed. It was restored in 1670 by an Act of Parliament, and at that time it was recalled that "Lighters, keels and other boats of considerable burthen", had regularly used it in earlier days.

Leave the stillness of Geldeston Lock, take the only track leading from the pub which weaves through low marshes, peopled by swans and lapwings, bisected by crystal-clear dykes. At the end of the track turn right onto the road, which is Station Road, and then right into The Street. Another picture postcard pub, 'The Wherry' stands on the left. Opposite here, there is a track by a phone box passing down the side of a hall. Before the boatyard the track bends left past the Garden House, a former pub. When the road bends further to the left, our route lies on the right through a small meadow towards Geldeston Dyke.

This narrow dyke is occupied by a host of different shaped craft in various states of repair. Walk under a low concrete bridge and continue walking further from civilisation along the edge of this wild enchanting dyke. To the left is a magnificent grazing marsh, low and prone to flooding, thereby attracting numbers of wading birds and wintering wildfowl.

The dyke kinks to the left and eventually joins the main river Waveney. The riverside landscape may not have the open character wherrymen would have liked, but the enclosed vegetation which has grown up around it gives an atmosphere of remoteness. There are no houses in sight; few boats venture this far, and the fishermen are well camouflaged and secretive.

At one point to the left is an area of damp swamp carr; a tangled area of boggy woodland, where fallen trees are entwined with undergrowth, brambles and berries, making it a riot of colour. The path leaves the river's edge for a short while turning through a shaded wood, resembling a tropical swamp. It then turns right again just before the start of a small slope. It follows alongside an old railway line to the left before skirting a private boatshed and returning to the water's edge.

As the cloistered woodland gives way to open marsh once again, Beccles tower stands tall and majestic on the horizon. Once back along the riverside settlement the gardens on the opposite bank of

A track across Beccles marshes

the river seem incongruously manicured and artificial after the wildness of the river stretch between Geldeston and Beccles.

The path along the river's edge in Beccles is clearly marked and at one point passes very close to the water's edge, before leading through a woodyard. At the main road, turn right over the bridge, and then next left towards the staithe. Here there are well-deserved ice-creams, a Broads Authority Information Centre, and a glorious open space next to the river to enjoy the lively scene. There is also some wonderful play equipment for the children.

At this point you can call it a day and walk back to the station. To do this, do not cross the bridge but continue on the road with the dyke on your left. This road bends to the right and comes to a T-junction. Turn left past a garage, and this then comes to a bigger T-junction. Turn right, which leads to a mini-roundabout and on the left is the station.

Alternatively you can explore Beccles Marshes, a huge area to the north of the town criss-crossed with well-trodden paths. The marshes, or fen as it was once known, was given to the people of Beccles in a charter granted by Queen Elizabeth I in 1584. The event is commemorated on the town sign which shows a humble resident of Beccles on bended knee before his queen. The marshes are an area drained for farming. Cattle were grazed on the marshes until about 1965 and some parts were then further drained to grow

Three wherries, in full sail, taking in the summer sun, and (left) a neglected tender taking in water

cereals, vegetables, sugar beet and horseradish. Today the marshes are leased to a farm company and a network of tracks and footpaths has been created, although the trails are closed every other Saturday afternoon between October 1 and January 31. The paths are indicated by yellow waymarks.

One attractive route to follow is the line of the Waveney. Walk through the park, past the play equipment and go under the road bridge. This riverside path takes you past a popular sailing reach and a popular stretch with fishermen who wheel contraptions resembling wheelbarrows to cart their gear to hidden reaches of the river.

The further the path wheels away from the town the more wild and isolated it becomes. Tall reeds and willow trees fringe the river edge and at times the open views are obscured by rampant growth of scrub and rogue woodland. At the northernmost point of the trail the path reaches what was once the Beccles to Great Yarmouth railway line which ran across the marshes until it closed in 1960. The pillars which supported the old swing bridge can still be seen in the river.

At this point it is possible to continue along the river edge and then turn right to walk along the Worlingham Wall, a bank built to carry water from higher ground to the river Waveney without flooding the land in between. The path we took turned right at the old railway bridge and followed beside the line of the disused railway before turning right again and weaving back towards Beccles bypass. As dusk approached we were treated to the sight of a barn owl hunting along the field edges.

Follow the trail to the road, passing close to some allotments and then cross over the main road at the roundabout. This road leads you straight back past a supermarket to the mini-roundabout, where you turn left for the station.

Berney Arms to Great Yarmouth

This walk starts in the heart of one of England's most precious grazing marsh landscapes, and weaves back to Great Yarmouth skirting Breydon Water, a tidal estuary which belongs to the birds and the boats of the Broads.

Start	Berney Arms Railway Station
Finish	Great Yarmouth Railway Station
⚓	Free 24-hour Broads Authority moorings at North West Tower, Great Yarmouth
👣	6 miles
⌚	2 hours
🧭	Landranger sheet 134

Berney Arms station

IT must be one of the most desolate spots to alight from a train anywhere in England. Berney Arms is the smallest railway station in England. It is such an isolated stop on the Norwich to Great Yarmouth line that you actually have to ask the guard to stop. On the other hand, if you're waiting at the Berney Arms platform, be sure to stick out your hand or the train could go sailing through. As the timetable puts it: "those wishing to join must give a hand signal to the driver".

The station was built in about 1843, only as the result of the landowner, called Berney, insisting on having a station there before he would agree to sell the land. But he made the error of not setting down that trains should actually stop at this station. In 1850 the railway company stopped calling at Berney Arms, and there then followed years of legal wrangling until services were resumed in 1855, and the court declared in Berney's favour five years later. So when you use this tiny station, tip your hat to a stubborn landowner called Berney.

To reach Berney Arms station, take a train from Norwich or Great Yarmouth, making sure it travels via Reedham, not Acle. Safely off the train at Berney Arms (the sign is almost as big as the platform), a walker could be forgiven for wanting to call back the train as it trundles off into the distance. For this is a daunting landscape, and it feels as if you have been set down in the middle of nowhere with only the cows and sheep for company.

Despair not. Look over the track towards the tall Berney Arms Mill, towering high above the River Yare. Cross the railway line and strike out across the grazing marshes towards the mill.

The silence is profound, broken only by the noise of cows, sheep and birds crying in the huge over-arching skies. If you scan the horizon with binoculars you should be able to count the remains of more than 20 windpumps, the most you can see anywhere in Britain.

The path threads through Berney Marshes, a nature reserve belonging to the Royal Society for the Protection of Birds, which has long been at the forefront of efforts to retain and restore wetland habitats. There is a lot of catching up to do. Drainage has been a feature of this country's landscape since at least the Bronze Age, and over the centuries gradual, creeping drainage has tended to go unnoticed. But it has been estimated that, between 1940 and 1981, more than 750,000 hectares, or 1.8 million acres, were drained or re-drained.

Clouds sail by moored yachts

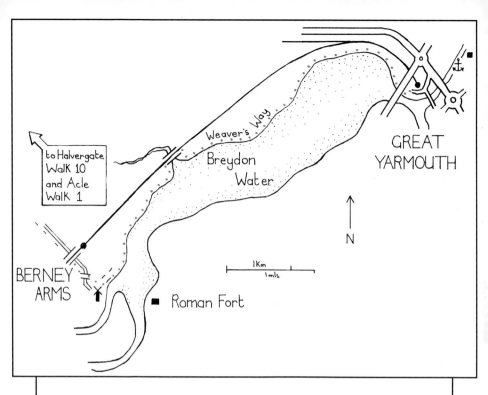

Berney Marshes were bought by the RSPB in 1985 when there was a threat of further drainage which would have upset the traditional way of looking after the marshes. The purchase of the land was a chance to establish a lowland wet grassland reserve — an opportunity which the first warden, Les Street, described as "too good to miss".

A survey of birdlife on the marshes confirmed that the decline in breeding and wintering birds had been severe. Drastic measures would be needed to reverse the effects of decades of damage, and a plan was devised to keep the Berney Marshes reserve much wetter, and therefore much better, than the rest of the surrounding land.

The RSPB has had spectacular success on Berney Marshes by carefully controlling when, where, and how much water is allowed onto the marshes. The results speak for themselves with vast numbers of over-wintering and breeding birds attracted to the area. In 1987 there were 700 Bewick swans, and 800 snipe, compared with 41 and 20 respectively before the RSPB regime took over.

Grazing is crucial to the RSPB's management regime. Animals are needed to keep the grass down, but their trampling feet have to be kept under control when there are eggs and small chicks about. Grazing is carefully planned; some *areas are tightly grazed to give short grass which is favoured by feeding wigeon and geese in the winter. Elsewhere the grass is left to grow longer for the benefit of nesting waders and ducks in the spring. Other areas are left ungrazed altogether to give longer grass used by short-eared owls.*

The best time to see birds on Berney Marshes is the most uncomfortable time — winter. Once the marshes have dried out in summer they are not so spectacular, but they remain beautiful.

Striking out across Halvergate Marshes towards the Berney Arms windpump

Eventually the path reaches Berney Arms Mill on the edge of the Yare. This is an impressive structure; framed against the huge sky with its vast sails gleaming in the sunshine, it is a landmark for miles around. At 70 feet, the mill is the highest in Norfolk, and did more than pump water off the marshes, for it also ground cement clinker for Reedham Cement Works. Numerous wherries would have moored up here to cart away cement cargoes. Take time to look around and climb up to the top for a glorious view. The mill, built in about 1865, is presently owned by English Heritage.

The path now follows the river bank and you need to turn left to head back towards Great Yarmouth. If your timing is good you can always enjoy a little liquid refreshment at the Berney Arms pub, a popular watering hole for holidaymakers on the river, and in the past a favourite haunt of wherrymen. The pub is closed in the winter.

Suitably fortified, continue along the river bank. Across the river you should be able to pick out the remains of the defence wall of Burgh Castle, one of a string of shore forts built by the Romans to guard against pirate Saxons invading their shores.

At this point the rivers Yare and Waveney merge to form the neck of Breydon Water, a 925-acre estuary, managed by the RSPB on behalf of Norfolk County Council. Here, grebes and diving ducks such as goldeneye can be seen in winter, and cormorants all the year round hunt fish, sometimes in the company of seals in the deeper water. When the tide is out the mudflats are host to quite different birds, with huge numbers of waders. Curlew, dunlin, oystercatchers, black-tailed and bar-tailed godwits, grey plover and ringed plover are among the many species which regularly visit. Every evening in winter a huge black-backed and black-headed gull roost numbering some 15,000 congregates.

In many ways Breydon belongs to the birds which both breed there and use it as a kind of halfway house when migrating. A local naturalist, Robin Harrison, devoted all his spare time for 30 years exploring the mudflats of Breydon and roaming the nearby marshes, wildfowling in winter and bird-watching in the closed season. From his houseboat *Lapwing* he observed and chronicled the changing moods of Breydon, a dynamic place which never failed to inspire him, and as you follow the winding path back towards Great Yarmouth it is easy to imagine Mr Harrison ensconced in his houseboat watching in the gloom of an evening as the birds flew in to spend the night on Breydon.

The path sweeps round to the left giving glorious views across the undeveloped marshes. Equally inspiring is the river view to the right. In the distance is the familiar skyline of Great Yarmouth with the elegant Breydon Bridge acting as a vanishing point for the flotilla of craft, big and small, heading to and from the port.

Breydon Water is a deceptive area of water. Its shifting sand and mud which disappears and reappears with the changes in the tide makes it a hazard for the unsuspecting crew of any holiday cruiser. Many is the cruiser that has been left high and dry on the sand until the tide turns, not least the cruiser belonging to the 'hullabaloos', the villains of Arthur Ransome's children's classic *Coot Club* which was set in the Broads.

The path skirts the edge of the estuary, leaving the main channel for boating over to the right. While the boats are fascinating to watch, it is something of a relief to leave behind the incessant droning of motor-powered craft and enjoy once again the silence of the marshes, interrupted only by the cry of a bird or the rattle of a train.

As you weave your way back to Great Yarmouth, the path almost touching the railway line but never crossing, the roar of the traffic gradually increases. With a tinge of sadness you leave behind the desolation of Halvergate and Berney Marshes to be greeted by the industrial beginnings of Great Yarmouth. The path, running between the railway line and Breydon, passes two bird hides which give good vantage points across the estuary. The lesser-spotted birdwatcher, complete with telescope and tripod, is a common visitor to these parts.

The path then passes under the concrete structure of the road and emerges, somewhat surprisingly, in the huge Asda supermarket car park.

Keep to the path beside the river, passing the supermarket car park on the left, and the railway station is signposted to the left.

The craft are more modern now, but sail power is still a popular way to enjoy the Broads

Brundall

People once believed that the Romans built and repaired galleys at Brundall. True or not, the legend lives on, and today boat building is synonymous with Brundall. This walk explores the riverside and then heads out of the village towards the surrounding countryside.

Start	Brundall Railway Station
Finish	Brundall Railway Station
⚓	-
👣	2 miles
⌚	1 hour
🧭	Landranger sheet 134

Brundall Gardens Broad in 1922, carpeted with water lilies. The gardens were once the destination of thousands of day trippers.

BRUNDALL was once one of the most fashionable destinations in the Broads. In the 1920s steamers packed with day trippers would moor up here so that passengers could explore the delights of Brundall Gardens, an ornamental paradise on the banks of the River Yare.

In 1922 an astonishing 66,000 visitors strolled round the gardens, many coming by train and alighting at the Brundall Gardens Station which was specially built to accommodate them; others came by bicycle, pony and trap, and on foot. Very few ever came by car. Yet 50 years later the gardens were little more than a memory. As W G Muter, the author of *A Hundred Years in Brundall Gardens*, puts it: "Year by year untamed nature had its way and choking weed growth and brambles invaded and gradually enveloped the steep slopes that characterise this most un-Norfolk-like place."

ℹ *The story of Brundall Gardens began in the 1880s when a prominent Norwich doctor, Michael Beverley, bought a holiday retreat in Brundall. A lake had been created when the embankment for the railway was dug. Dr Beverley planned* *and dug a further three ornamental ponds and in the course of this unearthed Roman artefacts. Archaeological scrutiny revealed the possibility that they were connected with Roman boat-building and repairing, creating the idea that the huge cleft in the hillside where the gardens were being created was once a Roman dock. This view has been somewhat discredited, but the Roman Dock name remains.*

Dr Beverley had a passionate interest in trees, and his vision must have been of an arboretum of spreading cedars, oak, yew, weeping willow, beech and ash. Today many of his trees still stand tall and proud and are home to a variety of birds and insects.

The estate was sold, and in 1917 there came on the scene one Frederick Holmes Cooper, a self-made man with more than his fair share of entrepreneurial skills. He was an estate agent by profession, and recognised the potential of opening up Brundall Gardens along the lines of today's stately homes. Cooper founded the Brundall Gardens Steamship Company to ferry visitors from the coast. As well as the gardens, he built a tea room, restaurant, and museum. People came in their thousands to stroll around the lake, marvel at the trees, and wonder at the skill and brilliance of Cooper's head gardener, Strachan.

Today Brundall Gardens is enjoying a revival under the careful stewardship of Mrs Janet Muter, who moved in to a modern house on the old site with a wild, untamed garden, only to discover it was a gardener's dream. Mrs Muter, with the help of neighbours and her husband Garry, has done wonders to restore the choked remnants of the gardens. The quality of the water in the lake is of the best anywhere in the Broads. Her aim is not to make it too formal, but to retain the wild character which Dr Beverley first envisaged. His surviving grandchildren, who have seen her efforts, have assured her that Dr Beverley would approve.

Although this walk does not pass Brundall Gardens, if you are in the area during Easter or the May Bank Holiday, it is worth checking whether the gardens are open. Information about opening arrangements will be found in the local paper, or in the *Gardens of England and Wales Yellow Book.*

The walk actually begins at Brundall Station, one stop along the line from Brundall Gardens if travelling from Norwich. If the Romans really did build and repair ships at the Roman dock, then today the tradition is alive and kicking a little further down river on the Yare. The station is in the heart of the boat building area of Brundall.

Walk towards the level crossing. The road goes uphill towards the village, but you need to turn your back on the village and head towards the site of activity — the boatyards. A long road takes you through the heart of the Brundall boatyard industry, passing yards with such fanciful names as Bounty Boats, and Bucaneer Boats, all building, repairing, maintaining, and hiring boats to suit every kind of sailor. Listen to the noises — the bangs, the

Brundall, one of the boat-building centres of the Broads

crashes, the shouts, the radios — it's a working environment. But return again as we did on New Year's Day and all you will hear is the chink-chink of ropes hitting metal masts.

As you walk down the road, the river is to the right, flanked by holiday chalets. Most are gaily painted, complete with the inevitable hanging basket, and their names reflect the holiday mood — Happy Days, Idle Hours and Anglers Rest.

The road ends at double metal gates and just before these on the right is a chalet named Ferry Lodge. Beside this is a passage-way leading to the river, at the end of which is a rather run down wooden landing stage. Look across the river to the Coldham Hall

Who pays the ferryman? A ferry across the river Yare once connected Brundall with Surlingham.

pub and you can see where the former ferry used to take its passengers.

Retrace your steps to the station, cross the railway line and then immediately turn right along a public footpath which runs parallel with the railway line. On the left the path passes a wooded embankment, modern houses, older houses with sweeping gardens, and a cricket pitch, while on the right is an area of tangled scrub and carr, and then a small private pond. At the end of the path turn left up a slight rise towards the main road. Cross the road, turn right and then immediately left into St Michael's Way, a residential estate. Keep following this cul-de-sac until it ends, where you will see a public

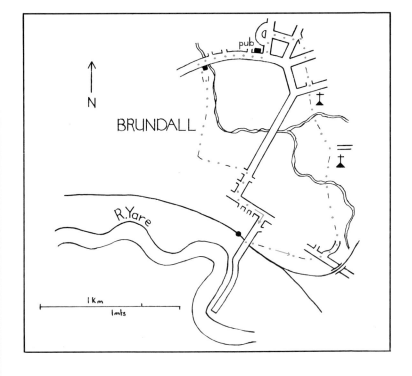

footpath sign to the right, running along the edge of a wooden fence.

In many ways Brundall is in the Norwich commuter belt. It was a trend which started as early as the turn of the century when retired and practising businessmen built residences here — Dr Beverley, who created Brundall Gardens, is an example of this. It was in the 1960s that the main development of new housing took place, and today the population stands at about 4,000, when 50 years ago it was about 300.

Here you can say farewell to the built up development of commuter belt Brundall, as the tree-lined path leads you between two fields, following the weavings of a stream. The views suddenly open out; behind, the roof tops of the houses are all that can be seen of suburbia, and ahead lies a glimpse of two churches. Keeping the stream on your right walk along the edge of the field until it leads you to a stile which takes you across the stream. When we walked here the cattle were curious but shy, and looked resplendent grazing serenely in front of Braydeston church.

Braydeston and Brundall were entirely separate parishes until December 24 1883, when they were combined for civic reasons under a local government order, and became known simply as Brundall. But Braydeston parish was retained, although in 1948 an attempt was made to merge it with Brundall and Witton. It was only the determination of the villagers, including supporters from

Brundall, which stopped this. The proposal would have turned the church into a chapel of ease, meaning it would lose its rights of baptism, marriage and burial, and it was felt the maintenance of the church would be neglected. They appealed to the only court available — the Privy Council. A two-day hearing was heard at Number 11 Downing Street before the Lord Chief Justice and two other judges, and the outcome was that although the amalgamation of the parish should go ahead, Braydeston church should continue as a parish church.

The path slopes up towards the church and then goes through the curious turnstile-type gate on the right leading into the churchyard. The church, dedicated to St Michael, dates mainly from around 1450, and occupies a lonely site on the Braydeston Hills. It is unusual in that the tower has a fireplace, and an oven in which the sacred communion wafers would have been baked.

Turn left out of the church gate, pass through a kissing gate and then turn immediately right following the public footpath sign across the next field. Straight ahead lies the next church on the walk, Blofield. This clearly defined path takes you across the field, through a gateway (no gate), and down towards the bottom of a tiny valley with the church on the rising land beyond.

Blofield church is in a lovely setting which can have changed little over the past hundred years. The path crosses a wooden bridge then goes through tangled undergrowth, more accurately over-growth because it is like walking through an arched hedgerow, until it emerges, after a stile, in the calm coolness of the churchyard. This church of St Andrew and St Peter probably replaced an older building on the same site. Its size and importance represents the prosperity the village enjoyed as a result of the wool trade. More recently in this century Blofield was renowned for the quality of its market garden produce. Brundall, too, was an area for produce, and its main entrance to the village from the A47 is called Cucumber Lane because of the fields of cucumbers and tomatoes which used to be grown under glass in roadside fields. Times have moved on and although the area is still renowned for its produce, it is now characterised by pick-your-own fields.

Taking the path leading out of the churchyard, turn right and walk along the road for 10 metres and then turn left up a path passing along the side of a private driveway. It turns from shingle to mud and comes out along the side of the playing field, home ground of Blofield United Football Club.

At the main road, cross straight over. Go through another kissing gate and follow the path, lined by a flint wall, which comes out once again amongst houses. Walk through this small development and the path emerges in The Street, opposite a small grocery store.

Turn left, and then right into Garden Road. At the end, turn left — don't follow the road to the right into Globe Lane — and keep straight on until you hit the main road. Turn right, past the front entrance of The Globe pub and strike out along what was once the main road into Norwich.

Pass the garage on the right, and just after this, cross the road and take the track on the left after the bungalow. Breathe the country air again as you walk along the edge of farmland, the mighty tower of Blofield church rising to the left.

The built environment beckons again and you quickly leave the open countryside. The path becomes more enclosed, with houses to the right, and it passes through a small wooded area to emerge on Brundall recreation ground.

The children will love this. Walk up the slight slope, and at the top is some of the best play equipment in the area, complete with strategically placed seat for Mum and Dad to enjoy the lovely view.

Swinging time over, continue on the path past the Brundall Memorial Hall and then take the signed footpath to the left running between two small fields, the land sloping down on the left. It comes out on a residential road, turn right, and then left at the junction with The Street. Turn right into Station Road to complete the walk where you started, at the station.

The first train to pass through Brundall was on April 12 1844; 30 years later a mail train from the station was involved in one of the worst accidents on the line. The mail train left Brundall for Norwich on what was then a single line. By mistake, a night inspector at Norwich allowed the Norwich to Great Yarmouth express train to leave after the mail train had already been given permission to depart. The trains collided between Whitlingham and Thorpe, both travelling at 35 miles per hour. Twenty-three passengers were killed, and the drivers and firemen of both trains, and many more, were badly injured.

It was as a result of this accident that the token system was introduced for all trains on single track. This meant that there was a tablet for each stretch of track, and unless the crew was in posses-sion of that tablet the train could not enter that stretch of line.

Bungay

Black-sailed wherries once regularly plied their trade to Bungay, but today boats no longer visit the town which nestles on the fringes of the Broads in the heart of the Waveney Valley. There is no railway station at Bungay any more, but buses run regularly from Beccles and Norwich.

Across the Waveney Valley. A view towards Bungay with the tall church tower and Bigod's Castle on the skyline.

Start	Bungay town centre
Finish	Bungay town centre
⚓	-
👣	8 miles
🕐	3 hours
🗺	Landranger sheets 134 and 156

BUNGAY lies in a sweeping loop of the River Waveney, standing proud like a sentinel keeping watch over the Norfolk and Suffolk border.

The River Waveney has through-out history brought turbulence and prosperity to Bungay. Romans, Saxons and Danes probably sailed up its meandering route, first to conquer and then to rule; and later it was the more peaceful black-sailed trading wherries which brought wealth, lining the pockets of a handful of well-to-do merchants.

The walk begins at the bus stop opposite the church and the Butter Cross. Grouped around here every Thursday is an open air market, in the shadow of the splendid perpendicular tower of St Mary's. Behind the bus stop is an opening signposted as leading to Bigod's Castle. Walk into the passage next to The Swan pub and the castle remains are on the right.

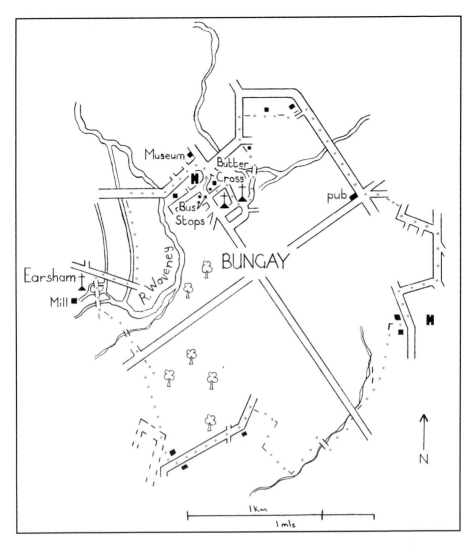

i *The original Bungay castle on the site is thought to have been built by Roger Bigod, who was something of a favourite with William the Conqueror. But in such turbulent times, Roger's son and heir, Hugh Bigod, did not find such royal favour. The story goes that he fortified the castle by building a square Norman keep with 18ft thick walls, rising to a height of 90ft. From this mighty stronghold Hugh Bigod's private army terrorised the East Anglian countryside, rebelling against Henry II.*

The king's patience wore thin and he marched on Bungay. Bigod surrendered without waiting to be besieged and the king ordered the castle to be destroyed. The king's men started tunnelling under part of the keep, but work was stopped when Hugh came up with a ransom.

The unfinished mine gallery remains and is one of the unique features of the castle. Hugh's days were numbered, and two years after he surrendered he was killed in Syria while fighting — ironically — for the king.

Wherry Albion *under full sail on the Broads.* Albion, *built at Oulton Broad, is the only trading wherry still afloat.*

It was another Bigod, Roger, who rebuilt the castle in 1294, the remains of which stand today. It was a peaceful time in the castle's history lasting 70 years. It was finally abandoned and the ruins passed into the ownership of the Howards, Dukes of Norfolk. In 1766 it was sold to a local builder who treated the ruins as a personal quarry, doing severe damage to the walls when extracting stone for road repairs.

Most of the castle then passed into the hands of Elizabeth Bonhote, wife of a Bungay solicitor who, wanting to live among the ruins, built a small house between the twin towers. It became her summer residence and source of inspiration for her novel writing, one of her books being called **Bungay Castle**. After her time there was further neglect and this continued for almost a century when, in 1934, a lease was obtained from the Duke of Norfolk to allow work to clear the vegetation and to excavate around the base of the central square keep.

Work came to a standstill when the £500 raised for the work had been spent. In 1962 Suffolk County Council bought a derelict sale-ground opposite the gatehouse and laid it out as part of the original inner bailey, and the masonry of the towers was repaired. The latest chapter was in 1987 when the Duke of Norfolk presented his ancient fortress to the town, and it is now looked after by the Bungay Castle Trust. A key can be obtained from the Gallery Bookshop in Earsham Street or the Cross Street Café, near the Butter Cross.

At the end of the path leaving the castle, instead of re-tracing your steps on the left back towards The Swan pub and the Butter Cross, turn right and then bear left along Castle Orchard to the

Footbridge near Earsham Mill in the Waveney Valley

wrought-iron gates at the entrance to Castle Hills. These were the outer earthworks of the castle, although built earlier by the Saxons as part of the town defences against the Danes raiding from the river-borne longships. The view at the top of these earthworks out over the meadows and river towards Earsham gives an inkling of why Hugh Bigod must have harboured delusions of invincibility.

Retrace your steps to the bus stop opposite the church, and then turn left, passing the Butter Cross on the right. This elegant structure was rebuilt in 1689 to replace the original which had burnt down in the great fire. Take a closer look at this monument, so called because farmers and market women would display their butter, eggs and other farm produce on the steps inside. It was also a place of correction and punishment; the stocks were fastened here, and there was once a cage for the detention of prisoners in the centre of the cross, although this was removed in 1836. The small dungeon which was beneath the floor was also later filled in.

On top, presiding over all, is the figure of Justice herself, and a particularly fine figure she cuts. It was bought by the town in 1754 for £29 13s 8d — possibly brought from London by sea and up river, since a further charge was made for carriage. Another curious feature of this justice is that, unlike many other traditional figures, she is not wearing a blindfold. The Bungay Justice is in good company, for neither does the justice on the Old Bailey in London.

Bear left at the mini roundabout. The houses along here are fine examples of solid Georgian architecture. A great fire practically destroyed the town in 1688, badly damaging both of the churches.

It is thought to have broken out in the Market Place at about 6.30 am on the morning of March 1. Within six hours its force was spent, but the damage it had wreaked was awesome — St Mary's Church, a grammar school, and many fine homes were badly damaged at an estimated cost of £29,898, the equivalent of more than £5 million today.

Pass out of the town, over a narrow road bridge crossing the River Waveney, bringing you out of Suffolk and into Norfolk. At the next bigger, less attractive bridge with iron railings, take the public footpath waymarked to the left. This leads between two meadows; to the left are the twin towers of the castle and the rectangular tower of the church, while ahead across the meadows stands the spire of Earsham church.

Walking along this low track on the very bottom of the valley it is possible to get a real sense of the geography of the area. The Waveney itself almost seems too small for its wide valley. This is not so far from the truth; the valley was cut by a river swelled by melting glaciers, making it wider than one cut by a river of the Waveney's present size.

The path follows the line of a dyke, quite wide in places, and there are gaps down to the edge where the cattle come to drink. Climb over a stile and then over a little wooden bridge which turns to the right heading towards Earsham church. The path is now narrower, surrounded by trees and hedgerows, and emerges onto a track.

Earsham is an ancient village, originally sited round the area near the mill and the church. Evidence of Saxon burials were found in a field opposite the church and it is also recorded that Vikings sailed up the river Waveney to attack the village. The church itself is thought to stand on the site of a Roman encampment.

Earsham is also famous for a special kind of nature reserve — the Otter Trust — which can be reached by continuing along the track past the church. It is about a mile further ahead on the left and is well sign-posted.

ℹ *The Otter Trust is run by Philip Wayre who has had consider-able success in releasing captive-bred otters into the wild. He has been breeding otters in captivity since the 1960s yet it was not until 1983 that the first release into the wild was made. It is a delicate operation. Otters have very precise habitat requirements and much of their natural river corridor has been damaged. The Otter Trust must be sure that each reintroduction has been preceded by a careful assessment of the conditions. The chosen river must have the right vegeta-tion and a healthy fish population. It must not be occupied already by other otters or mink, there must be little distur-bance — by boats for example — and agreements and*

*co-operation with the bank-side landowner needs to be
sought. And last, but not least, the young otter itself must be
carefully prepared and not be too attached to humans.
After release the progress of the otter is checked, in some
cases by the use of radio tracking. The greatest source of
satisfaction for the Trust is when the otter establishes itself in
the wild and subsequently breeds.*

The main route continues over the next bridge and then immediately left along a narrow path raised above the level of river and bordered by a wooden fence. Follow this path, crossing two more bridges, noting Earsham Mill to the right, then over a third bridge which crosses the Waveney bringing you back once again into Suffolk.

The route lies diagonally across the meadow, heading in the direction of the concrete bridge. In winter you can count many pairs of swans grazing on the meadow; they take a good look, but generally ignore you if you ignore them. At the bridge follow the sign which points diagonally right towards a gate and a stile, and thence to the road.

If you turn right along this road and walk for about a mile and a half, you reach the Norfolk and Suffolk Aviation Museum which has a collection of aeroplanes, equipment and memorabilia.

Cross the road and walk straight up the side of the field opposite. It is something of a short steep climb by Suffolk standards, but the more breathless you are, the longer will be your excuse for enjoying the view from the top. The path now basically follows the edge of what is a huge field. Turn right and follow the field edge, until it leads to the perimeter of what was once an airfield.

During the Second World War Earsham was at the centre of Allied air operations. Much of Earsham estate was used for the storage of bombs and armaments for the United States Airforce in East Anglia. There were eight airfields within 12 miles of the village, and next to the railway — now closed — was an area used as a marshalling yard for the unloading of bombs and fuel.

When the field meets the airfield road, turn left, keeping to the road, passing a farm on the left, and then about 20 metres further on, take a left fork cutting through a copse onto a road. Turn left, passing a big farmhouse. The road continues, surrounded by huge open arable fields, until it reaches a crossroads. Go straight over along the road marked 'To Farm Only'. Keep to this long lane until just before the farm gates when there is a stile on the right. It leads to a hummocky damp paddock at the end of which on the right is a wooden plank across the ditch taking you into the neighbouring field. The path is waymarked on the nearby tree.

Keep to the left of this next field heading slightly down hill once again. Follow the path as it skirts round a spinney and then continues to the bottom. Turn left following the dyke and then cross the dyke over a wooden bridge. Turn left again and continue between two fields until the path reaches a stile and comes out on the main road. Cross straight over and into the next field, crossing a wooden bridge. The path goes to the right of a long narrow field, at the end of which there is a track to the right.

This track is called Scotchman's Lane and is a former route leading to Mettingham castle. For many years this track was blocked and overgrown. It is shaded by gnarled hedgerows and trees, later narrowing and emerging on the road having passed a house on the right. Turn left along the road and keep a look out on the right for a glimpse of Mettingham castle. At the junction turn right and look for another view of Mettingham castle on this stretch of road. At the next junction take the left turn, signposted to Mettingham and Beccles.

Continue on this road for about 50 metres and then turn left onto a track, waymarked with a yellow arrow. This goes uphill again (who said Norfolk and Suffolk were flat!) and joins a road. Bear right, and when the road begins to bend to the right take the path leading straight down the edge of a field. Walking down this path, the view of the Waveney Valley gradually emerges once again.

The path comes out on the main road. Turn left and then cross the road turning right past The Watch Tower pub. Back on the valley bottom now, the road crosses the Waveney again near a mill and then over a further two bridges before passing Crisp's Maltings on the right. When the cottages end, and before the football pitch begins, look for a footpath sign on the left heading across the meadows. The path crosses a network of small fields and stiles, all well signposted, weaving its way towards Bungay. It leaves the fields and joins the road by a bridge. Turn left and follow this road into Bungay.

Were you to turn right along this road it would lead to the village of Ditchingham where Victorian writer and traveller Henry Rider Haggard once lived, from his marriage in 1880 until his death in 1925. Sir Rider was knighted in 1912, not for his novels, but for services to his country on Royal Commissions on subjects such as coastal erosion, reforestation and the study of agriculture here and in Denmark. His diary *The Farmer's Year* was written about his Ditchingham farm and estate and has been well read over the years. There is a delightful story about Sir Rider, who used to be a churchwarden at Ditchingham for many years. It is said that at the start of a sermon he would put a pile of half crowns on his pew ledge in full view of the pulpit. After 15 minutes he would remove a coin and so continue to do this at increasingly frequent intervals. What was left at the end of the sermon went into the collection plate!

Heading towards Bungay you pass a garage on the left. Fork left into Falcon Lane just before reaching a bridge. Go through the kissing gate which comes out at a lovely spot alongside the river, called Falcon Meadow. Cross the river at the weir and on the left is Bungay staithe.

ℹ *Bungay was once an important wherry building centre. Towards the end of the 19th century the navigation at Bungay passed into the hands of Bungay maltsters and merchants, W D and A E Walker, who owned a fleet of wherries, some actually built at Bungay staithe where they had their private yard.*

One of the best known wherry builders, William Brighton, began practising his craft at Bungay. He is most famous for the wherry Albion *which is still afloat on the Broads, owned by the Norfolk Wherry Trust.* Albion *was actually built at Brighton's yard at Oulton Broad in 1898 for W D and A E Walker. She is different from classic trading wherries in that she is carvel built — that is the hull is smooth, instead of being clinker built, where the planks overlap.*

It is thought that the Walkers stipulated this unconventional design specifically so she could negotiate the locks between Beccles and Bungay more easily, without snagging on the rough brick walls of some of the locks.

Brighton turned out a number of craft during his long career. Robert Malster, in his book Wherries and Waterways*, describes how Brighton began building at Bungay in his teens. In 1863 he turned out his first wherry, appropriately named the* Waveney*. She was built some distance from the river and had to be taken across the marshes on rollers to her launching. When he built his second wherry, the* Blanche*, she was carried through the streets on a trolley and launched sideways into a dyke.*

Turn right out of the staithe opposite a converted maltings and then keep right, joining Beccles Road. Pass a garage on the right and then take the right fork heading the wrong way up a one-way street.

Bungay has the curious distinction of having two churches almost next door to each other. The first is Holy Trinity Church on the right, a round-towered church which is the oldest building in Bungay. On the outside of the old door is a small brass plate commemorating the quenching of the great fire on this spot in 1688.

In contrast, a little way further on the left is St Mary's, felt by many to be the architectural centrepiece of Bungay, with its soaring tower which can be seen for miles around. The church is first mentioned in 1183 as being part of the Benedictine nunnery. The ruins of the priory, dissolved in 1536, can be seen as you walk through the churchyard.

For centuries the two churches were maintained in use side by side, at one time sharing a common churchyard. Two separate parishes were formed, and this situation survived until this century. In 1947 a united benefice was formed, bringing the churches into a single parish, although both buildings continued to be used for services. But in 1977 inflation reared its ugly head and it was recognised that the situation could no longer continue. With much regret St Mary's was declared redundant, and was taken on by the Redundant Churches Fund in 1981, which has since undertaken extensive maintenance and restoration work.

The path through the churchyard brings you back on to St Mary's Street almost opposite the bus stop where the walk began.

Sailing on the river Bure

*Rails across the water. Reedham swing
bridge.*

Cantley

This walk through the country lanes and grazing marshes of Cantley is dominated by the huge sugar factory. It is a factory with a fascinating history, and is sited in the heart of some stunning wetland scenery.

Start	Cantley Railway Station
Finish	Cantley Railway Station
⚓	-
🥾	6 miles
⏱	2 hours
🧭	Landranger sheet 134

The looming presence of Cantley sugar beet factory on the river Yare

THE village of Cantley on the river Yare is dominated by the ever-looming presence of a vast factory.

Cantley Sugar Beet Factory is part of British Sugar plc and has been the only industrial feature on the Broads landscape since the factory was constructed in 1912. Anyone applying to the Broads Authority today for permission to site such a complex on the marshes would doubtless be laughed out of committee. While no-one would suggest Cantley factory has merged with the landscape, it has evolved to become part of the scenery, and serves as a graphic reminder that the Broads is a working landscape where people have to make a living.

The station itself is under the shadow of the factory. Turn your back on the factory entrance and walk up Station Road leaving the factory buildings on your right. At the height of the sugar beet harvest, known locally as the 'campaign', a constant stream of about 600 lorries a day pours through the village into the factory gates, sometimes forming a queue of at least 30 lorries stretching back over half a mile. The lorries, the mud on the road, the stray beets which tumble from the lorries, and the smell (something akin to roasting marshmallows) which permeates the surrounding area, have become part of the way of life.

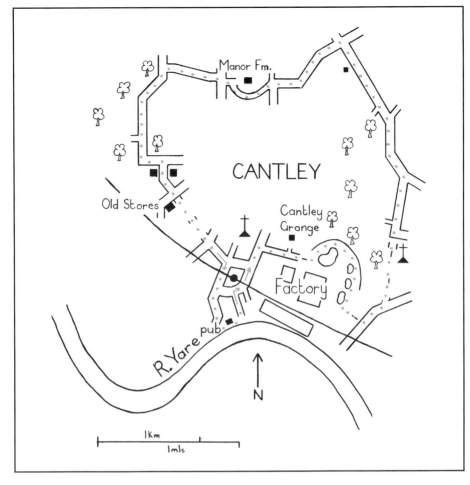

i The story of the Cantley Sugar Beet Factory begins with the vision of a Dutchman, one Jerald van Rossum who was convinced that Norfolk and Suffolk, with soils and weather similar to areas of Holland, were perfect for growing sugar beet. Cantley was chosen as the ideal site for two obvious reasons; the river Yare and the main Norwich to Great Yarmouth railway line. Building began in 1912, at a cost of £170,000, although to guard against failure, more than £500,000 was invested abroad in Dutch sugar, which proved to be a shrewd move.

The factory itself was fitted out almost entirely with second-hand machinery and equipment shipped from a factory in Holland and transported up river by wherry, or by rail. Building the factory was no easy task. Contemporary newspapers reported serious riots taking place, probably because of communication difficulties between Dutch, British, German and Austrian workmen working flat-out to complete the factory in nine months.

The early days were not a success. Production did not meet expectations, the factory opened at a loss. Those teething troubles were compounded by a shortage of growers as more and more people were called up for the First World War, and in 1916 the factory closed. In 1921 the English Beet Sugar Corporation re-opened the factory and in 1922 it made a profit. Sugar beet had arrived in Norfolk.

Pass the lorry entrance on the right and just after this turn right into Grange Road, a track lined with oaks, from which the hum of the factory can be clearly heard. Cross the stile and where the track forks, continue straight ahead on the grassy path. This skirts the perimeter of the factory through curious landscapes. There are huge earth mounds on the right, and signs tell you to avoid dangerous ponds, making it all seem rather like a castle moat. On the left is a dyke, thick with reeds and beyond is tangled carr woodland, giving the impression of nature lapping at the fringes of the factory.

Keep following the line of this dyke until the heavily-wooded land on the left becomes a more open field punctuated by several large willow trees.

On the left is a wooden bridge over the dyke. Cross this and follow the path in the shadow of the willow trees until it meets a larger track. Turn left and follow this track for about 45 metres until you see a stile on the left. Cross the stile and take the wide grassy path leading through an enchanting avenue of trees which gradually closes in, passing to the right of a wood. The thick undergrowth is excellent cover for pheasants, so don't be alarmed when they squawk and fly across your path.

The track continues round to the left, but your way lies straight ahead between two high hedges forming a corridor which emerges onto a minor road. (It is worth taking a short detour to the right to visit the tiny church of St Botolph, Limpenhoe, with its squat tower and long, low chancel.)

Turn left onto the road and the route lies along minor roads, lined with thick hedgerows, which in autumn are bursting with blackberries. Fields flank the roads, many of which doubtless include sugar beet in their crop rotations. Farmers growing sugar beet in the early days were very much pioneers, and there were few willing to take the risk of trying an untried crop. The factory had great problems getting enough beet to process. Records show that on the very first day of processing, November 11 1912, Cantley dealt with 372 tonnes of beet. Most modern factories would see that off in about 90 minutes. Today at the height of the campaign, Cantley processes anything up to 7,500 tonnes of beet each day, but averages about 6,800. In a year it will process roughly one million tonnes.

It plays an important part in the local economy with a permanent workforce at Cantley of 230 rising to about 410 during the processing campaign. To the 1,026 farmers supplying the factory it pays about £30 million a year. In terms of sugar this equates to about 950 to 1,100 tonnes of sugar being produced every day. It is unlikely that you would stir it in your tea, since the sugar from Cantley is mainly used for bulk supply to the food processing industry, although some does find its way direct to the shelf in the form of Silver Spoon icing sugar. Make you feel hungry?

Pass a road on the left, and at the next T-junction turn left. Bear left again at the next junction, and then look out for the ruins of a church on the left. The remains, crawling with ivy and undergrowth, have an eerie quality about them, and the absence of obvious gravestones heightens the curious atmosphere about the place.

Go left at the next junction, and carry on to Manor Farm, where the road bends sharp left, but you need to take the small by road which forks right off the bend and leads past the front of the farm. Be sure not to miss the two magnificent sweet chestnut trees.

The road meets a bigger road which you need to cross by way of a staggered junction right then left. Follow this narrow lane until it turns sharp right. Then take the track to the left which dips down and follows the edge of a field with carr woodland to the right. As this path continues there are good views across the marshes towards the river and railway line, before the path curls to the left up a slight rise to rejoin the road by a group of farm buildings. Turn right down the hill and at the bottom there is a junction. Cross over and take the path which goes to the left of a house called The Old Stores.

The view of the river and marshes re-emerges on the right, while up ahead beckon once again the huge storage silos of the sugar beet factory which have dominated so much of the skyline on this walk.

At the end of the path cross straight over the road into Malthouse Lane. After having replenished provisions, if necessary, at the Post Office and shop on the right, carry on until the road leads into Church Road. Bear right again towards the level crossing and cross the railway line. Follow the road until it starts to bend left and at this point strike out straight ahead along a concrete track towards the river, ignoring the dead-end sign.

The track takes you between open fields, where lapwings and sheep graze, towards the slightly raised river bank. At the Anglian Water pumping station the concrete road ends and the path leading to the river bank turns to grass.

Once on the river bank, pause and look across the marshes from this vantage point. In winter they will be teeming with birds and wildfowl. To describe the landscape as flat would be something of an understatement; but flat it is, and quite stunning too. Apart from the factory there are hardly any vertical features to break the monotony of these marshes, which gives them a particularly melancholic air. In winter the marshes will probably be teeming with birds, their cries competing with the drone of the nearby factory.

Turn left along the river bank to face the factory and head towards the Red House pub. The Yare, which flows from Norwich to Great Yarmouth, was once the main transport route for the factory and carried huge cargoes of sugar beet feed. This is the by-product of the factory — a high-energy animal feed sold in pellet form.

The factory still uses the river for transporting some of its products, and a regular caller is the tanker *Blackheath* bringing fuel to the factory. During the campaign, coasters call at Cantley and make a return journey to Great Yarmouth port, laden with their cargo. For anyone hitching a ride on one of these vessels it offers some of the best views in the Broads. Riding high on the bridge, it is possible to see over every river bank across miles of grazing marsh and to get an almost eye-level view as the coasters negotiate Reedham Swing Railway Bridge. The unusual sight of a huge ship on the river is enough to make any holiday cruiser scurry for cover.

Turn off the river bank passing down the right hand side of the pub along a track heading back towards the village. This emerges almost opposite Cantley station.

As you head for the station it is worth musing on the fact that this was once a transport artery. In mediaeval times Norwich was a thriving city, ranked third in the country, and many supplies and commodities to meet the demands of a wealthy city came up the Yare from Great Yarmouth. The river could not be negotiated by the large seagoing vessels and the goods had to be transferred to wherries. When sections of the route were subsequently dredged and regularly managed it was possible for larger vessels to make the trip.

In 1991 a remarkable era of navigation came to an end. As part of a new bypass round the south of Norwich, a huge viaduct across the river Yare had to be built. It meant the days of unrestricted access from the sea to Norwich were over. It was something of a sad day, and when the mighty girders were winched into position to span the river, there were a number of sailors and navigation enthusiasts there to witness the historic occasion. One particular regret was that tall ships would no longer be able to make a regular trip to Norwich, but in reality the days of busy commercial activity at Norwich had all but ceased.

Martin George, in his book *Land Use, Ecology and Conservation of Broadland*, explains that there was a revival of commercial activity on the Yare from the First World War onwards. Cantley Sugar Beet Factory was part of the reason, receiving coal and beet

Wherries at the Red House pub, Cantley

by water, and exporting pulp and molasses. But most of the traffic in the early 1920s was as a result of the Boulton and Paul engineering factory establishing a base at Norwich riverside. In 1923 there were 101 seagoing vessels visiting Norwich, generating an income in tolls of £204. This peaked in 1936 when 753 vessels used the port, many of them serving a coal-fired power station in Thorpe. The last collier ship arrived in 1970 shortly before the Thorpe plant closed and since then the number of ships declined. In 1988 just seven ships visited the city.

Oulton Broad and Carlton Marshes

From the bustle of Oulton Broad to the tranquillity of a Broads microcosm, this walk takes you from a popular holiday destination to the wilder retreats of the Suffolk Wildlife Trust's Carlton Marshes Nature Reserve. The walk can be done either from Oulton Broad North Station, or Oulton Broad South. The North Station is on the Norwich to Lowestoft line, while the South Station is on the Ipswich to Lowestoft line.

Start	Oulton Broad South or Oulton Broad North Railway Station
Finish	as above
⚓	Oulton Broad Yacht Station (tel. 0502 574946)
👣	4 miles
⧗	1½ hours
🧭	Landranger sheet 134

Power boat racing on Oulton Broad

OULTON Broad found its true identity during the Edwardian era when the well-to-do would flock to the wide expanse of Oulton Broad and take part in glittering regattas, once prettily known as 'water frolics'.

Wealthy gentlemen who owned fast, sleek racing craft would employ a professional helmsman to look after the craft and sail her during the season, chasing what was sometimes big prize money, but more important was the glory of winning; albeit a very local glory. The helmsmen were often allowed to keep any prize money they won which could amount to a tidy sum at the end of a successful season.

Racing still takes place on Oulton Broad but times have moved on, and it is now the only venue in the Broads where power boat racing is allowed. Throughout certain designated evenings and weekends in the summer the peace and rusticity which writer

71

George Borrow once experienced at his home on the edge of Oulton Broad is shattered by the roar of mighty horse-power outboard motors.

This walk starts at either of two stations — Oulton Broad North, or Oulton Broad South. The former is on the Norwich-Lowestoft line, the latter on the East Suffolk line running from Lowestoft to Ipswich.

Starting from Oulton Broad North, turn left out of the station towards the shops and houses — not towards the roundabout and the garage. This leads through the main street towards the bridge marking the boundary between Oulton Broad on the right, and Lake Lothing on the left. Follow the path by the cycle track which takes you down through an underpass at river level and emerges almost next to Mutford Lock which has been restored. Its double-mitred gates make it unique and there are plans to site a Broads Information Centre close by.

Mutford Lock, gateway to the Southern Broads

ℹ *Mutford Lock represents an important landmark in the history of trade in the Broads and was constructed largely as a result of a bitter, long-running dispute between Norwich and Great Yarmouth.*

In the early part of the 18th century Norwich was said to be the country's third city, ranking in wealth and trade only behind London and Bristol. But all cargoes in and out of this busy city had to come through Great Yarmouth, being transhipped from seagoing vessels to wherries and keels, because none but the smallest of the seagoing craft could navigate the Yare. Great Yarmouth was able to derive thousands of pounds a year in tolls levied on imports to the port, and Norwich became increasingly angry at its rival's refusal to improve the channel across Breydon Water to allow bigger seagoing vessels to gain direct access to the city.

In an age of great engineering activity a group of irate Norwich businessmen sought an alternative solution. A consultant engineer, William Cubitt, was commissioned to find a way of making the river navigable for seagoing vessels right up to the city. His first scheme was rejected, and instead he came up with the idea of creating a new navigation between Norwich and the sea at Lowestoft which would bypass Great Yarmouth altogether. None other than Thomas Telford was brought in to comment on the proposals, and while he said both were feasible he urged Norwich and Great Yarmouth to work together for their own best interest. No chance; instead the rivalries of hundreds of years came to the surface. When the scheme from the Norwich port lobby was defeated in Parliament there was general rejoicing in Great Yarmouth. But it was short-lived, and in 1827 a new bill passed safely through Parliament giving the sanction for the Lowestoft to Norwich navigation to be created.

The scheme included the creation of a new cut linking the river Yare with the Waveney at Reedham and Haddiscoe, and the building of Mutford Lock which would enable seagoing vessels to move between Oulton Broad and Lake Lothing regardless of the state of the tide. The whole scheme, whilst technically feasible, was ill-fated. The cost rocketed and when it was eventually opened with much civic celebration, it was well-used for the first couple of years but was never the missing link needed to make Norwich the seagoing port it wanted to be.

After crossing the footbridge next to Mutford Lock, turn right and stroll along The Boulevard, close to the water's edge. Here there are day boats to hire to explore the Waveney, and also passenger cruisers to take you on a short river tour. On the left is what must be the only thatched harbour master's office in the country, and here the official notices about the dangers of rabies are a reminder that Oulton Broad is a gateway to Europe.

Pass through the iron gates at the end of The Boulevard and this brings you into Nicholas Everitt Park, a grand area of open space with children's play areas, an outdoor swimming pool, bowling green, tennis courts, Lowestoft Museum, trampolines, hungry ducks and seats from which to just sit and watch the activity on the broad.

The park was bequeathed to the people of Oulton Broad through the generous offices of two friends — Nicholas Everitt, writer and sportsman, and Howard Hollingsworth.

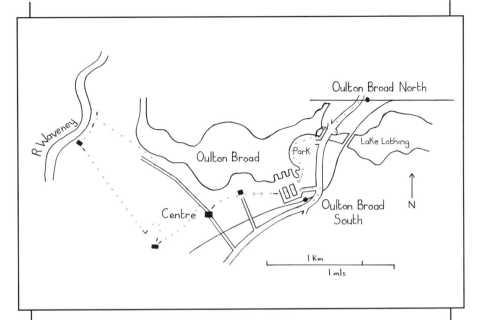

Hollingsworth ran a successful business in London, but his heart belonged to Oulton. His lifelong friend was one Henry Reeve Everitt, a lawyer, who lived at Broad House overlooking the broad. Described later in a local magazine (*Norfolk Fair*) by a junior clerk in his firm as "urbane with a touch of military style discipline", it came as no surprise to the clerk, one R W Moore, to learn that Everitt had been engaged on "secret service missions". His claim to local fame came about under the pen name Nicholas Everitt, writing books on the subject of wildfowling in the Broads. When Everitt died in 1928, his friend Hollingsworth took the chance to secure a lasting memorial to his friend's memory by buying the entire estate which went with Broad House, 15^1/2 acres, and giving it to the borough for the benefit of the townsfolk on the condition it was called The Nicholas Everitt Park.

It was a grand gesture, and today the park remains somewhere for informal recreation where holiday crowds bask by the side of the broad to watch sailing events, water skiing and power boat racing. Hollingsworth was honoured by being made the first honorary freeman of the borough.

Follow the path through the park, passing the sailing club on the right, crossing a wooden bridge and going through a gate. The path then veers away from the broad, passing between a slipway and a large thatched wooden boat shed. Keep to the path and follow it round the edge of a mooring basin. Cross the footbridge and walk through the car park, passing Pets Corner on the right. On reaching the main road turn right and after 20 metres take a slip road on the right which dips down and emerges to the right of Oulton Broad South station. Walkers starting from this station will join at this point. The slip road divides into three. The left fork passes directly in front of former railway buildings, the middle fork goes to a holiday camp, and the right fork is a track. Take this track which leads past Marsh House. When the track bends sharply to the right and towards the broad, our route lies straight ahead along the waymarked footpath which passes through a caravan and chalet park. Keep to the path as it crosses various chalet park roads and then passes between two fields — the larger to the left and a smaller paddock to the right. Cross the stile and walk through the field to the next stile. Follow the path round the edge of this field and then head straight for the Suffolk Wildlife Trust's visitors centre which should be in view straight ahead. The path emerges in the visitor centre car park. The centre is well worth a visit.

In many ways Carlton Marshes is a microcosm of the Broads. Within its boundaries are many of the typical broads habitats — open water, reed beds, carr woodland and grazing marshes. Its dykes are some of the cleanest in the whole Broads. In summer they are the haunt of dragonflies and damsel flies which hover and flit from stem to stem. The grazing marshes are vivid with the colours of wild flowers our grannies once picked for fun, but which sadly have disappeared from many places through herbicides and modern farming practices.

Round Water in the heart of Carlton Marshes
Nature Reserve, a microcosm of the Broads

In winter Carlton Marshes has a desolate quality. The flowers of summer have gone and in their place are wading birds and wildfowl which come to feed on the rich pickings of the grazing marshes.

The Suffolk Wildlife Trust acquired Carlton Marshes Nature Reserve in 1980 at a time when much of the surrounding area was being drained and turned over to agriculture. The reserve covers some 45 hectares and much of it is a Site of Special Scientific Interest. The management regime is geared towards encouraging and supporting wildlife. The marshes are grazed in summer by cattle; no chemicals are used to give plants such as marsh orchid and ragged robin the chance to grow. The fens are cut on a cycle designed to give a variety of conditions to encourage a wide range of plants.

The visitor centre has displays showing how the marshes were looked after in the past, and what is being done today. In school holidays the Suffolk Wildlife Trust runs children's activity days to introduce children (and their parents) to the wildlife of the reserve. The centre is open on Sundays throughout the summer and on many weekdays. Numerous paths criss-cross the reserve and it is possible to explore the varied habitats of the marshes. No set route is suggested here because half the fun of a visit to Carlton Marshes is discovering your own route around this beautiful corner of the Broads.

To return to the urban hum of Oulton Broad, retrace your steps along the footpath from the visitors centre car park, back through the caravan and chalet park to Oulton Broad South station. Walkers who joined here may want to take the chance to stroll around Nicholas Everitt Park, while walkers from Oulton Broad North station will need to re-trace their steps around the park to return to their starting point.

Cromer and Felbrigg

This walk starts in Cromer, the seaside capital of North Norfolk, but heads away from the sea towards the stately grandeur of Felbrigg Hall where the elegance of another more graceful age is invoked. The walk is characterised by spectacular woodlands, the foundations of which were laid several centuries ago.

Start	Cromer Railway Station
Finish	Cromer Railway Station
⚓	-
👣	8 miles
⌚	3 hours
🧭	Landranger sheet 133

Cromer Pier, home to one of England's last remaining end-of-the-pier shows

AS you pull into the seaside town of Cromer, alighting almost at the check-out of a modern supermarket, it is worth remembering that the coming of the railway was in many ways the making of Cromer.

From about 1785 Cromer was visited by several families of retired habits whose favourable reports soon attracted others. It became a fashionable, select sea-bathing centre, with a daily coach from Norwich via Aylsham.

But in 1877 the Norwich to North Walsham railway line was extended to Cromer, putting it within reach of a much wider cross section of society. The holiday trade grew quickly, not to everyone's approval, as one contemporary observer commented "hotels of a size and magnificence that make the dwellings on the cliff seem humble in comparison, adorn, perhaps too well, the unpretentious coastline, like jewels on the dress of a simple village maid".

Although the walk begins in Cromer it does not take in the town itself. It is well worth exploring; the museum in Tucker Street gives a glimpse of the town's cultural and social past, while the climb to the top of the church tower, which at 160ft is the tallest in Norfolk, gives a panoramic view of the North Sea. Cromer has a close association with the sea and has a proud history of unstinted bravery from its lifeboat crews who have been launching to save others since 1804. Henry Blogg, the most decorated lifeboatman ever, became a national hero through his life saving.

This walk, however, heads away from sea, towards the stately splendour of Felbrigg Hall. Turn left out of the station, heading downhill towards the town, but turning right into Hall Road, on the corner of which stands the Methodist Church. A recreation ground is on the left, and from here the Weavers' Way long-distance footpath is signposted. Like our route it follows the main road, passing a belt of trees on the right and an open field on the left.

Just past a gatehouse on the right is a Weavers' Way sign into a field. Take this, keeping to the left edge of the field and then crossing the field towards the right. The waymarking then points you to the left, passing to the left of a small copse. At the corner of this copse, continue diagonally towards the railway bridge at the corner of the field.

Cross the red brick railway bridge and continue into the next field following the left edge. Keep to this field edge until it winds its way to the top left hand corner of the field, and an opening through a hedge. Walk down the few steps onto a road which is dwarfed by huge trees. Turn right and then about 20 metres on, turn left along a narrow path, sign posted for the Weavers' Way. The path starts off enclosed but then the countryside opens out with a field on the right. It narrows again close to a flint barn and turns into a concrete road. This joins the main road. Turn right until you reach the tiny Felbrigg village green and a war memorial.

Take the track to the left of this, leaving the main road, still following the Weavers' Way signs. The track ends at a gate just past some classic flint cottages. Cross the stile, and this time ignore the Weavers' Way sign which goes to the left, instead go straight across the field towards a bank of trees and turn left when you join the road which then sweeps round to Felbrigg Hall.

"The spring is always cold and late on the Norfolk coast. For weeks at a time the wind blows in from the sea, a chill drying wind, northerly or easterly. The trees — horse chestnut, sycamore, beech, oak, sweet chestnut — come slowly into leaf under a reluctant sun. It is long before the blades of corn even begin to hide the tilth from view." So wrote Richard Ketton-Cremer, the last private owner of Felbrigg Hall, a Jacobean house which, in the ownership of four families, saw remarkably little change.

🄸 *Richard Ketton-Cremer, the last private owner of Felbrigg Hall, inherited the hall from his father, who in turn had inherited it from his eccentric uncle, Robert Ketton.*
Richard was later to write a history of Felbrigg and in that book, Felbrigg. The Story of a House, *he records that when his*

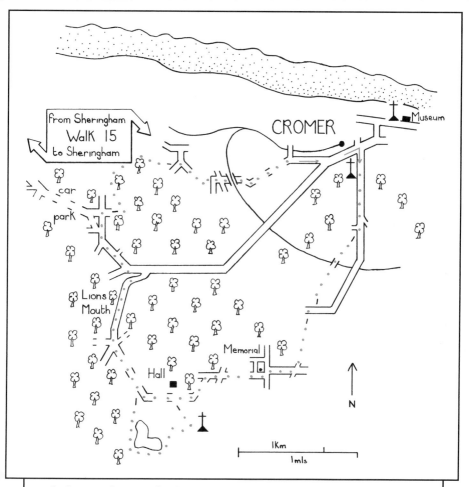

father took over the house in 1924, it was as if the house had
been slumbering for half a century. There were no bathrooms,
and water was still raised from a well by a huge wheel
worked by a mule. There was no heating, no lighting, no
power and no telephone. The roof was in a fearful state; death
watch beetle had taken hold in great areas of roof timbers.
The gardens, too, were in a sorry condition, while the church
on the estate was in a shocking state of repair.

The house had originally been built by the Windham
family who had established their seat here in the 15th century. Various alterations were made through the generations.
In 1863 it was sold to John Ketton, a successful Norwich
merchant who had made his fortune out of oil-cake and cattle
feed. His purchase of the hall — lock, stock and barrel — was
quite a talking point at the time. It then passed to a younger
son who died without heirs, and so came to his nephew who
was the father of Richard Ketton-Cremer.

Richard's parents moved in and slowly and steadily started to bring the estate back into shape, lovingly tending the gardens and woodlands, a traditional paternal management which Richard himself was to continue when he inherited Felbrigg in 1932. Affectionately known as the 'Squire', he continued to update the house, installing electricity in 1954, and finally central heating in 1967 — although only in the modest flat which he adopted as winter quarters. But his pride and joy were the woods and there is scarcely an acre on the estate today which has not received the benefit of his planting. When Richard Ketton-Cremer completed his history, the future was not secure for his beloved house. He ends his story of Felbrigg: "and so it stands, with all its associations and memories, confronting the unpredictable future. It may be the scene of happiness, kindness, hospitality in centuries to come. It may be burned to the ground this very night. The story of its first three and a half centuries has now been told; and who can know what lies ahead?"

On his death in 1969, Richard bequeathed the hall and estate to The National Trust.

The National Trust has laid out two walks around the estate, one taking in the lake and the church, the second through some of the estate's beautiful woodland.

To find the start of the lake-side walk, go past the front of the hall, keeping it on your right, and turn left at the cattle grid. This leads you through a small wooded area, which was planted about 200 years ago both for commercial purposes and for landscape value. A group of wild cherries, beautiful when in flower, were planted for their impact, while beeches were planted for commercial cropping. Some beeches still survive, though they are rather aged and windblown. Other species in this block include sweetchestnut, lime, and sycamore, while cherry and holly are the only species which would have been found in a local mediaeval natural woodland.

At the end of the wood, cross the stile and follow the line of the fence to the next stile. At this second stile the wire fence at right angles to the path divides the valley into two grazing lots. The lower one is more like a traditional pasture, while the one just passed through has been more intensively managed with fertilizers and herbicides.

Take the path between the two post and wire fences and follow this to the right-angled bend where there is the first view of the lake. This was formed in the 1750s when the valley was dammed and small ponds excavated for fish farming were merged into one lake. For this was the age of landscape gardening, when any self-respecting

(left) Fishing boats hauled up on Cromer beach

estate owner felt the need for a semi-natural lake in his overall vision for his estate.

Cross the bridge and follow the path which leads round the lake.

There is almost a mini-wetland environment around the lake. Here is to be found the richest diversity of wildlife on the Felbrigg estate. Over 50 plant species have been recorded in this relatively small area, such as marsh marigold, ragged robin, yellow flag and reedmace, none of which are particularly rare. Many of these have disappeared from the low-lying meadows around Felbrigg because of drainage and more intensive farming.

After the open water the reed bed can be seen, then the walk passes through an area of alder carr, rich in insect life. It is thought that the alders here were probably once coppiced. This would have been done once every ten to 15 years and the hard, dense poles would have been used to make charcoal.

Emerging from the wood, the path turns left along the top of the dam. Among the wildfowl on the lake are a regular flock of Canada geese, which were introduced to Britain as ornamental birds. The Felbrigg flock is wild and flies several miles each day to feed on the nearby salt marshes. Leaving the lake and following the line of the ruined wall, the land is much drier now. It is an area of permanent pasture, and in general has been managed organically, without fertilizers or herbicides.

Continue walking up the hill and towards a clump of young oak and beech trees. These were planted in the Queen's Jubilee year of 1977. The path follows the edge of fields towards the tiny, isolated Felbrigg Church, a humble building in which a number of the great and mighty of the Felbrigg estate have ended their days. It was probably once the heart of a village community, but people disappeared from the original settlement and there is little to suggest when and why. Most of the structure today is the work of Sir Simon de Felbrigg who rebuilt much of the church in the 15th century.

The path back to the hall goes diagonally through the parkland which is beautifully surrounded by sweet chestnuts, beeches, sycamores and oaks. The chestnuts would once have been in straight lines, forming rectangles — a passion from Tudor times when the fashion in gardens was for formal lines and symmetry. At Felbrigg around 1750, this formal pattern was changed as the fashion for sweeping, natural parklands took hold.

The Woodland Walk is clearly marked and leads through some of the oldest and best documented woodland plantations in the county. Leaflets about both of the walks are available from the National Trust.

🛈 *In 1680, about 200 years after the Windhams came to Felbrigg, William Windham (I) started some of the first British tree plantations. Windham clearly had a passion for trees. His* favourite was the sweet chestnut, introduced by the Romans who brought the species from the eastern Mediterranean because of its edible nuts. These chestnuts have thrived at Felbrigg, replacing oaks as the dominant parkland trees.

Felbrigg Hall Lake, home to a regular flock of Canada geese and other wildfowl

Many of Windham's operations on the estate are recorded in his 'Green Book'. In that, he writes that in 1676 he planted a nursery "which I hope will bee carefully preserved, soe long as it please God to continue it in the familye". It was no mean nursery either; in it he planted acorns, ash seeds, holly berries, haws, maple and sycamore seeds, beech mast and chestnuts, besides 4,000 oaks and about 2,000 other trees. These trees would have been subsequently used for planting on the estate — to make a copse for the deer, and to enclose particular areas.

Trees and woodlands clearly calmed the soul of William Wyndham. When in later life he was embroiled in politics and defeated in an election, he wrote of the far greater delight which he took in "my Nursery and Garden". As Felbrigg historian Ketton-Cremer wrote: "I cannot help wondering whether ... he was thinking of his well-filled nursery of children, or of his more tranquil and more tractable nursery of young trees."

The tradition of woodland management continued. Another William Windham (III) placed the management in the hands of Nathaniel Kent, a professional agent and agricultural improver, whose books make regular reference to Felbrigg. The Great Wood was expanded with a mixture of evergreens and deciduous trees, including Scots pines and silver birches. The Felbrigg Scots pines used to support a dense population of red squirrels. These creatures nest in tree tops and do not hibernate. They obtain, instead, a source of winter energy from pine seeds which are rich in oil. Grey squirrels, on the other hand, do hibernate. They were introduced only about 100 years ago at a time when the population of the red squirrels was falling. The grey ones now dominate. At Felbrigg, grey squirrels only arrived in the late '70s,

Stately splendour of Felbrigg Hall, which is in the care of the National Trust

but since then their red counterparts have all but disappeared. Visitors are now asked to report any sightings of red squirrels. The last owner, the Squire, was also passionate about trees, and the thriving state of the Felbrigg woods today is largely his achievement. As many as 200,000 trees are thought to have been planted by him over 40 years, many of them in Victory Wood. With its two great rides forming a V-shape, it was conceived as a memorial to Victory in Europe Day.

Having fully explored Felbrigg and its magnificent woodlands we must start to leave, following the way out signs to the road. Turn right here and the road passes through 'The Lion's Mouth' which is still part of the Felbrigg estate. The name is apt, since there is a feeling of walking through the jaws of a woodland, and being devoured by tall straight trees, reminiscent of a lion's teeth. The texture, colour, shape and smells of the trees are magnificent, and it is something of a disappointment when you emerge from the gully on to the main A148 Cromer to Holt road. Cross the main road and take the narrow road opposite, also lined by trees and woods.

Follow this road, which bends to the right, and then joins another road. Keep right until it reaches the entrance to the National Trust Roman Camp and Beeston Regis Heath. This is described in the walk from Sheringham (15) and a detour to this area is worthwhile.

Turn off the road to the right and then take the first path which forks to the left. It is marked low down on a post with a yellow arrow and long-distance path symbol. This takes you down into a gravel gully, shaded on either side by trees and also rhododendrons. The track turns to a path running between a grassy area to the left and a field to the right. At the junction of paths continue straight, through the kissing gate, following the line of a hedge on the right of a field and take a tiny bridge over a stream. Cross a small patch of scrub and the path joins a track. Here the route lies left and then immediately right, up a track lined with trees and hedges. It is slightly uphill and track quickly turns to path. It curls to the left and then joins a track on a bend. Bear left passing some farm buildings. Cross straight over the road and go under a brick railway arch and continue up the track called Stone Hill.

At the top of this track through a gate on the left is another glimpse of the sea, a welcome view after the enclosed walking in shaded woods. Ahead lies the church tower of Cromer. Near the railway line the track turns into a road. Bear right and the road comes out amid modern houses on the outskirts of Cromer. This joins the main road, and a little way down on the left is our starting point, the railway station.

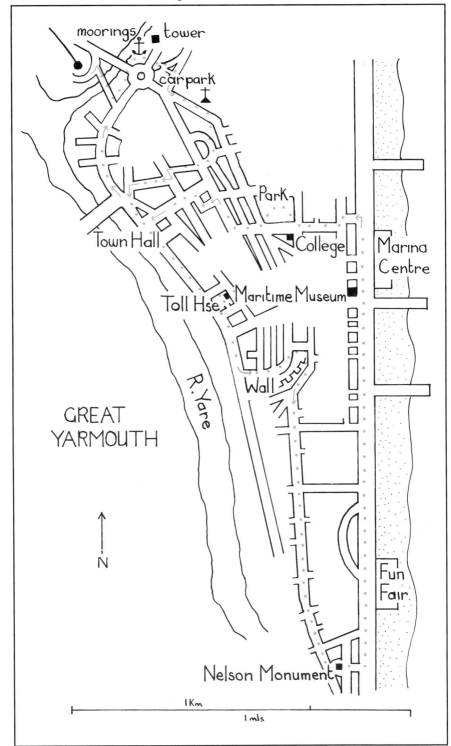

moorings tower

carpark

Park

Town Hall

College

Marina Centre

Toll Hse.

Maritime Museum

Wall

GREAT YARMOUTH

R. Yare

N

Fun Fair

Nelson Monument

1 Km

1 mls

Great Yarmouth

Unravel the enigma of Great Yarmouth with its stomach-churning thrills and spills, behind which lies a community founded on shifting sands. Today there is a famous fun fair, yet there was once a famous mediaeval herring fair, and at the turn of this century Great Yarmouth was the herring capital of the world. This walk traces the history of Great Yarmouth, and reveals a port steeped in culture and tradition.

Start	Great Yarmouth Railway Station
Finish	Great Yarmouth Railway Station
⚓	Free 24-hour Broads Authority moorings at North West Tower
👣	8 miles
◇	2½ hours
🖼	Local street plan

"I see no ships"... The traditional sun, sea and sand holiday is alive and kicking in Great Yarmouth.

BRASH, loud and garish in summer; strangely empty and deserted in winter; Great Yarmouth is an enigma in the county of Norfolk. It has a quite different atmosphere from any other part of the county, save perhaps King's Lynn, and there the clue lies. For both are ports and the population of both have for many generations depended on the sea.

Great Yarmouth is built on a sandbank which gradually formed during Roman times across the mouth of the great estuary known as Gariensis. The surrounding sea was heaving with fish, and it is likely that the settlement probably began as a seasonal camping site where fishermen could pull up their boats and dry their nets. Gradually it became more permanent — merchants and traders probably moved in — so that by 1086 there was a small borough of about 400 people.

Marooned as it is on one of the most easterly points of the country, Great Yarmouth has always proved something of a wild card; the joker in Norfolk's pack. Alfred Hedges, a local historian puts it this way in his book *Great Yarmouth as it was*: ..."its men were free from most of the irksome restrictions of the feudal system. They were merchants, seafarers, fishermen and pirates. They were no tillers of the soil and owed no allegiance to a Lord of the Manor, for the town was owned by the King."

With that declaration of independence ringing in our ears, we set off from Vauxhall Railway Station. Turn right over the pedestrian bridge across the river. Known as Vauxhall Bridge, this is the place where many a holiday cruiser comes a cropper, mis-timing their run under the bridge and losing a windscreen, or at worst getting stuck until the tide ebbs once again.

Turn left at the main road and head towards the roundabout. Go under the subway which takes you down to the level of the river, under a low bridge. Ahead is the North West Tower, once part of the town's formidable defences, now a Broads Authority Information Centre and well worth a visit. Leaving the Centre, retrace your steps slightly and turn left into the next section of subway. Continue straight, leaving a car park on your right and head through a rather uninviting narrow alley which emerges on Northgate Street opposite St Nicholas Church.

Cross the road and turn right walking round to the front of the church, dedicated to St Nicholas, the patron saint of mariners. Over the years, as the town has increased in prosperity, so the church has grown. By the 19th century it was claimed to be the largest parish church in England. It was heavily restored in the 19th century so little of the original is visible. In the war it was badly damaged. Hit by the Luftwaffe in 1942, the spire tumbled and a richly carved pulpit was completely destroyed.

Nestled close to the church, next to the Old Vicarage, is one of the prettiest buildings in the town. It is the house where Anna Sewell, author of *Black Beauty*, was born in 1820, and is now a restaurant.

Cross the road at the pelican crossing and bear left towards a courtyard of tiny houses. This is the Fishermen's Hospital, built by the Corporation of the day in 1702 to house 20 fishermen and their wives aged 60 and over, who had fallen on evil days. They are miniature works of architectural art.

Not missing the canon mounted opposite the hospital, continue through the market place, and you will pass number 68, the erstwhile home of one Miles Corbet who died in 1662. Corbet, MP for Great Yarmouth and the town's Recorder, was a rebel who supported Parliament during the Civil War. Such was his allegiance to Cromwell that he was one of the signatories of Charles I's death warrant. At the restoration he fled to Holland but was arrested in 1662 and sent back. He was condemned to death for high treason and hanged, drawn and quartered at Tyburn.

The market has always had a high reputation and was once thought to be one of the largest anywhere in the country. In 1879, Ernest Suffling, advising would-be holidaymakers to the Broads, recommended Great Yarmouth fruit market as one of the finest in England. Today it comes alive on Wednesdays and Saturdays, and also Fridays during the summer season. Jellied eels and cockles are a speciality, and the chips, hot from the vans and wrapped in white paper, are unrivalled.

Cross the market place and go down an alleyway called Market Row. Today this alley is little more than a curious shopping street, paved, lined with shops and somewhat dingy. But imagine a town consisting almost entirely of these rows, lined with houses, back-to-back, no natural light, set out on a grid system, reminiscent of America and its blocks. This was how Great Yarmouth was built. All building had to be done within the rather narrow confines of the town wall, only about 133 acres, so the houses had to be built as closely together as possible. These 'rows' were badly bombed during the Second World War but those who can remember living in them recall dark, dingy places, where there was no natural light and little privacy. To start with the rows were all named, until 1804 when they were numbered to avoid confusion. Some had pictur-esque names, like Snatchbody Row, near the churchyard, named after body-snatchers Vaughan and Murphy who had a house there in the early 19th century. The narrowest row was Kitty Witches Row which at one end measured only 30 inches across.

At the end of Market Row, cross over and continue into Broad Row. Turn left at the bottom and this takes you out onto the quay.

As you stroll along the wide pavements of Hall Quay it is not hard to imagine the wealthy merchants patting their fat pockets, as they strolled along the same route 100 years ago. Then the traffic would have been all horse-drawn and the skyline would have been dominated by the rigging and masts of fishing boats lined stem to stern along the quay. Today the skyline is punctuated by cranes, pylons, warehouses, silos, and modern steel ships.

Pass around the front of the Town Hall and then turn left along South Quay. Defoe is reported, in *Great Yarmouth: History, Herrings and Holidays*, to have said that the town had "the finest quay in England if not in Europe", and that "among the buildings were some merchants' houses which look like little palaces". Number 4 South Quay, one such palace, is now a museum of domestic life and social history. It was originally built by a wealthy merchant, Benjamin Cooper, in 1596, but had a number of prominent owners, not least one John Carter who was a personal friend of Oliver Cromwell. Rumour has it that the fate of Charles I was discussed in an upper room.

Row 92 leads you to the Greyfriars Cloisters, where the Franciscan Greyfriars once occupied a site. Turn left down Gaol Row, number 106, which leads past the entrance to the library and then turn right and immediately on the right is the Tolhouse. This impressive 13th century flint building was the hub of civic life for centuries. It served as the court of the borough and also as the gaol from 1261 until 1875. Borough Council meetings were also held in the Tolhouse until the present Town Hall opened in 1882. The council then decided to demolish the Tolhouse, but thankfully a respect for the past prevailed and the building was restored by public subscription.

Over the years the gaol housed vagrants, debtors, criminals and prisoners-of-war. In one particularly grizzly episode in 1645, Matthew Hopkins, the infamous Witch-finder General, condemned 16 women as witches and they were held in the Tolhouse gaol before their execution.

Just past the library turn right along Row 111. Here a fine example of a merchant's house has been preserved and tours can be arranged. Turn left on re-joining the quay. Today it is characterised by the big ships servicing the gas rigs and transporting cargoes across the North Sea, but this would once have been a mass of fishing drifters. If it was a Sunday early this century then you would have been able to walk across the river from Great Yarmouth to Gorleston stepping from boat to boat. For no self-respecting fishermen, especially the Scots, would ever dream of working on the Sabbath.

The fishing industry started in Anglo Saxon times. Fishermen and merchants were attracted to the area by the rich harvest

The fish wharf at Great Yarmouth. By 1900 the port was the herring capital of the world .

that was to be had, and this seasonal influx of visitors gave birth to one of the great fairs of mediaeval Europe, the 'Free Herring Fair'. French, Dutch, Scandinavian and Italian boats came to fish and the fair lasted from Michaelmas to Martinmas. Herrings were an important foodstuff in mediaeval Europe; they were nutritious and kept well if they were smoked. Great Yarmouth herrings were supplied to monasteries, the royal household, and to feed troops. Many were exported and records show that in 1344, 60 foreign vessels loaded up with cured herring during just one week.

The fishing industry expanded rapidly in the 19th century. Better vessels were developed with gaff rigs, and the coming of the railways meant faster distribution of the fish. A new fish wharf was built in 1869 which meant catches could be landed more easily and then sold. It was also earlier in this century that a new way of curing herrings was discovered, supposedly by a curer named Bishop. It was a lightly-smoked 'bloater' and was to become forever associated with Great Yarmouth. Today the football team bears the nickname The Bloaters.

But by far the biggest impact on the fishing industry came from the influence of the Scots who started coming from the 1860s. They would work their way down the east coast, arriving at Great Yarmouth in the autumn. They brought with them important changes; the Scots had developed a way of gutting herring and then pickling them in brine, and towards the turn of the century the export of pickle-cured herring overtook the traditional smoked red-herring trade.

They also brought with them hundreds of Scottish fisher-girls and curers needed to gut the fish, pickle them and pack them. While they were waiting for their menfolk to bring in the catch they would busy their fingers with knitting, and when it was time to work, their sleeves would be rolled up and their strong forearms engaged in gutting and cleaning millions of herring.

By 1900 Great Yarmouth was the premier herring port in the world. The wharfs would be strewn with wicker baskets to unload the catch, and packed with barrels ready for pickled herrings; with merchants waiting for their boats and with the fisher-girls lining up ready to prepare the catch. Not only was it an industrial boom, it was a social phenomenon. It has been estimated that the fishermen, the girls, the curers and coopers swelled the town's population by 10,000 during the season.

The Scots also added to the fishing revolution by introducing the steam drifter. Viewed with some scepticism at first, they quickly superseded sailing drifters. Steam boats brought a fundamental shift in the pattern of fishing. They were *expensive to buy and operate, and instead of family-owned boats they became part of company fleets. This was the heyday for the industry. Record-breaking catches were landed, and on one day in 1906 there was such a glut that fish had to be sold as manure, and for the first time some boats even returned to dump their catch at sea. In 1913 about 1,000 vessels fished from Great Yarmouth, catching and selling herring worth about £1 million.*

We can only speculate how it all would have continued had it not been for the First World War. A total of 179 drifters from the Great Yarmouth fleet were requisitioned by the Admiralty. Some were used to man anti-submarine nets in the Dover Straits and the Adriatic. Others were used for patrol, minesweeping and examination duties. The losses were significant — 17 drifters were lost, three by direct enemy action.

Optimism was high after the war and the fleet actually grew to its greatest size in 1921, when 1,149 vessels fished from Great Yarmouth. But the world picture had changed. The Russian and German markets on which the industry had become so dependent had collapsed. The death knell sounded when the Scots gradually stopped coming. The Second World War meant a second round of war service for some requisitioned boats. Afterwards the fishing was resumed on a smaller scale with motor drifters ousting steam, but by the mid 1950s it was becoming obvious that fish stocks were seriously depleted. In 1963, the last six boats which remained of the local fleet were sold and the period of Great Yarmouth's involvement in the great herring fishery was over.

Aside from the herring trade, Great Yarmouth had retained its place, along with King's Lynn, as a thriving port. Trade tended to fluctuate depending on international relations, but alongside imports and exports there grew up an important ship building industry which was to last well into this century. Today the port is mainly concerned with the offshore gas industry.

We now leave the quay and turn left towards the sea into Friar's Lane, passing the fire station on the right and heading towards the old town wall. It turns into Trinity Place and leads to Great Yarmouth Potteries housed in an old herring smoking works.

Turn right down the cobbled slope and then right again following the line of the wall. This wall was built in recognition of Great Yarmouth's importance as a port in mediaeval times. The town had a history of providing sea-faring men and ships to help in the protection of the realm, and it was vital that such a town should be properly protected. Work began on the wall in 1285 but was not complete until about 1485, when it had eight gates and about 15 towers. Each citizen had to do their bit either working in person or by paying someone to do their share. Today almost two-thirds of the wall survives, including 11 towers and turrets, making this one of the most complete mediaeval walls in England.

Blackfriars Road (where you are walking) is probably the finest stretch. Keep on this road, which turns to Camden Road, and then cross over at a crossroads into Admiralty Road. On the left you pass St Nicholas Hospital. This area, known as the Denes, was an undeveloped area of sandy heath until the end of the 18th century. The wealthy tradesmen who controlled the town corporation feared competition from a new commercial area outside the walls, so forbade development. But nevertheless the first building was an army barracks during the Napoleonic Wars. The first barrack master was Captain Manby, an eccentric genius who invented a line-throwing mortar, the precursor of the modern rocket apparatus used to rescue crews from shipwrecked vessels.

This long stretch takes you through a residential area with streets named after characters of Dickens, in respect of the author's association with the town. Admiralty Road eventually leads, appropriately enough, to Nelson's Monument, a towering construction completed in 1819 in honour of Norfolk's most famous sea-farer.

Nelson was actually born at Burnham Thorpe in North Norfolk, going to school in Norwich and North Walsham, and persuading his father to allow him to go to sea at the tender age of 11. After finding fame but little fortune (he was never well off) on the high seas, Nelson made three fleeting visits to Great Yarmouth. In 1800 he landed at the town after the Battle of the Nile in 1798, where he had commanded a fleet, and in a night raid captured or destroyed 11 out of 13 French ships of the line.

Great Yarmouth treated him like a conquering hero. His carriage was drawn by the crowds from the beach to the Wrestlers Inn in the Market Place where he stood at an upper storey window with Lady Hamilton to receive the adulation of the people. He was presented with the freedom of the borough, and it was at this ceremony that a rather flustered town clerk administering the oath asked Nelson for his right hand. The withering reply came: "That is at Tenerife."

His second visit was in 1801 when he was preparing to sail for a campaign in the Baltic. A year later, after the campaign, he again landed at the jetty in Great Yarmouth but this time ignored the ceremony arranged for him and went instead straight to the naval hospital on the Denes where many of the wounded from his campaign were lying.

On his death, a tribute was clearly needed by Norfolk for its most famous hero. A monument was decided upon and a coastal location was thought the most fitting place. Built at Great Yarmouth, it would have the dual function of being a seamark. The whole structure is 144 ft high and a small viewing platform at the top can be reached by a staircase of 217 steps. It was originally to have been crowned by a Roman galley, but Britannia was later thought to be more suitable. She faces inland towards the harbour.

Jack Sharman was appointed caretaker for the monument, and had the right sort of background for the job. At the age of 14 he had been press-ganged into the navy while working at the Wrestlers Inn. He joined the Victory *under Captain Hardy and claimed to have helped carry the fatally wounded Nelson to the cockpit. He came to be keeper of the monument in 1817 after being discharged from the navy and admitted to Greenwich Hospital. Dickens is supposed to have visited Mr Sharman at the monument and modelled the character of Ham Peggotty on him in* David Copperfield.

Continue past the monument towards the seafront and turn left. In front now lies the new face of Great Yarmouth with its seafront amusements, rides to thrill, fast-food, and fast money-making ideas. Seaside holidays became fashionable in the second half of the 18th century when sea water was recommended as a universal cure. Great Yarmouth quickly took advantage and built a Bath House on the Denes equipped with sea water baths and assembly rooms for balls and tea parties. In those early days visitors were attracted by the quaint rows, the houses and fishing industry as well as by the sea.

The railways brought new visitors to Great Yarmouth and were instrumental in turning the town into the resort it is today. It opened up the town to visitors from the industrial Midlands, a tradition which continues to the present day. Many mining families from the North and the Midlands made an annual pilgrimage to Great Yarmouth, and when the miners' strike was going on in the 1980s Great Yarmouth was one of the resorts to feel the pinch.

In response to more visitors, the town allowed more holiday-related development. Marine Parade, the main seafront thoroughfare was finished in 1857, not long after Wellington Pier was built. The Winter Gardens which embellish the entrance to the pier were bought at a bargain price from Torquay where they had originally been sited from 1878-81. The second pier, the Britannia, was built in 1858, at the northern end of Marine Parade.

Great Yarmouth has never been slow to follow the holiday fashions. Aquariums have come and gone, and presently come again; a revolving tower was once the main attraction; cinemas and theatres have been adapted and turned into bingo halls or other weird and wonderful attractions. Famous names in show business have performed in summer seasons — Charlie Drake, Leslie Crowther, Frankie Howard and more recently Michael Barrymore and Jim Davidson have topped the bills.

In straining to meet every conceivable need of the holiday industry, Great Yarmouth can never be accused of being unimaginative. In the mid '80s someone even suggested tethering a redundant gas platform at the end of one of the jetties as a tourist attraction. And then there was the question of whether or not the horses pulling open carriages up and down Marine Parade should be made to wear nappies. This one floundered in the council chamber.

On Marine Parade, a little way past the jetty on the left is the Maritime Museum, dwarfed by amusement arcades and leisure centres. This unassuming building, once a home for shipwrecked sailors, houses much fascinating history and many traditions of Great Yarmouth.

Turn away from the razzmatazz of the seafront into Trafalger Road which leads to the College of Art and Design. Cross the road here and walk through St George's Park, past the war memorial, and leave the park through the top left exit. Bear left which brings you out between St George's Theatre on the left, and the Methodist Church on the right. The former was once a church modelled on Wren's design for St Paul's Cathedral and paid for by a special tax on imports of coal into the port.

Turn right into King Street, and then walk down left through the covered shopping arcade. This bears right, and then turn left heading towards the river once again.

i *Great Yarmouth harbour, or haven as it is better known, proved a challenging engineering task for successive generations. For centuries the entrance to the harbour silted up, forcing all but the smallest ships to unload at sea. In 1347 Edward III gave permission to cut a new outlet nearer the town to give an entrance to the harbour. This was to be the first of seven attempts to create a stable harbour. The expense over the next 200 years was to cause the town severe financial embarrassment, despite grants from successive monarchs.*

In 1559 all the town's inhabitants were ordered to help build a new cut, and when the river broke through the new harbour works, a Dutch expert was summoned to oversee the work. The price was high, but the scheme worked and the seventh haven survives until this day.

Turn right at the Town Hall to re-trace your steps along Hall Quay. Once past the bridge (don't cross it) follow the route of the main road running closest to the river which leads back to the Vauxhall Bridge footpath and back to the station.

Berney Arms - Halvergate - Berney Arms

If solitude, silence and sweeping skies are your inspiration, then this walk through the heart of Halvergate Marshes is a must. It can either be a circular walk from Berney Arms, or from Berney Arms to Acle.

Halvergate Marshes

Start	Berney Arms Railway Station
Finish	Berney Arms Railway Station or Acle Railway Station
⚓	-
👣	6 miles
⌚	2 hours
🗺	Landranger sheet 134

THIS walk takes a bit of planning because it starts and finishes at Berney Arms Station, the smallest railway station in England, where trains are not exactly frequent. But with the aid of a current British Rail timetable it should be possible to time your walk so you catch a train either back to Great Yarmouth or on to Reedham or Norwich.

When you get off the train (don't forget to tell the guard), with your back to the train, turn left and walk to the end of the platform. Across to the left you should see Berney Arms Mill. Turn away from this and follow the footpath to the right which strikes out across Halvergate Marshes.

Once the train has trundled out of sight and sound, just stand a moment and soak up the atmosphere. Doubtless Noel Coward would find it 'flat', but for many this expanse of grazing marsh is an awesome sight. The nearest road is two miles away and you feel for all the world that it is just you and the elements. The infinite skies, like moving pictures, have inspired many artists and the scenes they have painted (many can be seen in Norwich Castle Museum) have changed little since the 18th century.

i *Halvergate Marshes is the largest area of grazing marsh left in eastern England. But it was nearly lost altogether. For over 300 years cattle, sheep and horses have used the marshes as summer grazing. Cattle were even walked all the way from Scotland to be fattened on these marshes, before being sold for beef in London. Daniel Defoe passed this way in 1722 and described the grazing cattle as "monstrously fat".*

Man has always sought to drain the marshes, first by digging dykes to take the water off the land to the rivers, and later by building drainage mills, or windpumps. Windpower was replaced by steam and eventually by diesel pumps — hence the abandoned stumps which were once majestic mills with turning sails.

The traditional grazing regime meant that Halvergate was an ideal habitat for wildlife, especially waders, wildfowl and other wetland species. In spring and summer these include redshank, yellow wagtails, lapwings, oystercatchers, shoveler, snipe and mute swans, and if you are lucky a marsh harrier. In winter hosts of duck and geese fly in to feed on the desolate marshes.

But in the 1980s, this unique habitat was threatened by progress and changes in European farming policy. Farmers were being encouraged, by means of grants and subsidies, to drain grazing marshes and plough up the land to plant more cereals. On Halvergate it came to a head in 1986 when the marshes became the centre of national attention. Already a quarter of the marshes had gone under the plough and the Broads Authority, determined to protect a traditional Broads landscape, stepped into the fray.

The only way would have been for the Authority to pay compensation to farmers for not ploughing up their marshes. The high sums involved would have quickly bankrupted the Authority. Instead they drew up an experimental scheme whereby the Government paid farmers £50 an acre for managing the marshes in a traditional way. It was a major breakthrough and the first time that the Government had paid farmers for conservation-led farming. It proved to be the forerunner of the Environmentally Sensitive Areas Scheme which gave farmers financial incentives for farming in a traditional way which protected the countryside and wildlife.

The path reaches a stile (Weavers' Way should be waymarked), and then the path goes straight across a field towards a small bridge over a dyke. Ahead is the slight rise of Wickhampton and Halvergate, behind you the huge expanse of the marshes.

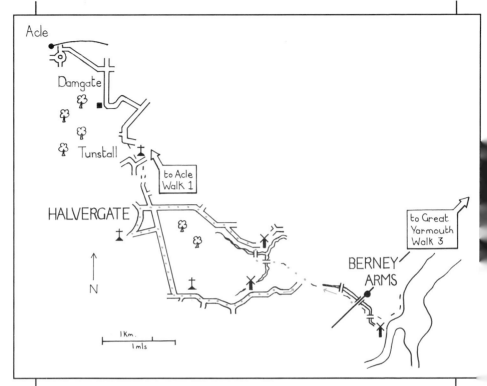

After the bridge, head diagonally and right across the next meadow towards a concrete bridge; a windpump and white painted farmhouse should be to the right. Cross the bridge and then follow the farm track round to the left, again heading towards Halvergate. The track follows the line of a drainage dyke and then comes to a very muddy end as it goes past a cattle pen.

The track reaches a road. Turn left towards the village and should you feel the need of refreshment then stop for a break in the thatched Red Lion pub, on the right.

If no rest is required, carry straight up what is becoming a definite hill in Norfolk terms. About 100 metres on the right is a turning called Squires Road, next to a post box. This route leads to Acle and the directions are given at the end.

To complete the circle back to Berney Arms, continue straight until the road forks. Take the left fork and follow this until you reach the village sign and war memorial. Then double back along the street, passing the post office on the right, until you reach a T-junction. Turn right to Wickhampton and follow this long country lane past the playing field on the right. To the left, on a clear day, there are views across the marshes, and if you're lucky you can see all the way to Great Yarmouth.

At the next T-junction turn left towards Wickhampton Church. If you go in here you can read about the legend of Halvergate and Wickhampton and how they got their names. Take the concrete track that passes to the right of the church, signposted 'Marshes Only', and head once again to the silence and vastness of Halvergate Marshes.

The dykes are thick with reed and willow; in summer the dragon-flies and butterflies flit and hover from plant to plant; in winter the silence is broken only by the cry of rooks circling overhead. At the junction of the concrete track turn left. Straight ahead is Berney Arms windpump and further along on the right is one of many derelict windpumps.

In the past, these marshes would have been the haunt of marshmen, a special breed of men who worked the pumps, checked the cattle, kept the dykes clear, and kept a watchful eye on hundreds of acres of marsh.

i *Drainage of the marshes started in about 1750. Early mills would have been small wooden smock mills which were later replaced by brick tower mills, often on the same site. They worked huge scoop wheels, and later pumps, to lift the water from cuttings in the marsh to higher channels and then into rivers where it would flow into the sea. By the middle of the 19th century, when drainage was widespread, the drainage mills would have dominated an otherwise empty skyline. At one time there were probably about 200 mills working in the Broads, and about 20 were still being used in the 1930s. The marshman would look after the mill, keeping an eye on the water levels, usually living in a tied cottage close-by, or occasionally actually in the mill itself.*

Towards the end of the century, progress came along in the form of more efficient steam and oil-driven pump engines, and the days of the wind-powered drainage mills were num-bered. Their death knell was sounded with the introduction of electric pumps which could do the work of dozens of drainage mills at the press of a button, and had no need to rely on the vagaries of the weather.

Just how wet the Halvergate Marshes would have been without drainage is illustrated by a report written in the 1780s by one William Marshall, who reported on the rural economy of Norfolk. He describes riding through Halvergate Marshes: "For nearly the first mile we rode to our horses knees in water."

The path weaves back to join once again with Weavers' Way. This time turn right, and re-trace your steps back towards Berney Arms Station.

To walk from Berney Arms to Acle, turn off right 100 metres past the Red Lion pub in Halvergate into Squires Road. This leads

Brooding skies over the ruins of Tunstall church

past a former school and cottages. Ignore the footpath on the right, and continue straight across the fields. To the right from here are glorious views towards Great Yarmouth. With binoculars you can pick out many landmarks, including several drainage mills; white sails can be seen making slow progress along the Bure, and the glinting metal of cars as they journey up and down the Acle straight.

The track ends but the path continues straight along a grass footpath, still raised between two fields. Just coming into view to the left is the ruined church tower of Tunstall.

As the path nears the end of the field it dips steeply down to join the road. Turn left, following the sign post for Weavers' Way, towards the church. Take the concrete track to the right, again sign posted Weavers' Way, which passes within touching distance of the deserted church tower, inhabited only by crows and rooks. A footpath leaves the concrete track almost level with the tower, heading straight across the field. This again is sign posted for Weavers' Way.

This well-maintained grass path dips slightly and at its end joins a road. Turn left and keep on this path for nearly a mile until it reaches a track to the left, sign posted for Weavers' Way. Turn left down here and follow this track as it weaves its way between fields until it reaches a big metal gate and cattle pen leading to a grazing meadow. Climb the stile and follow the track towards the barn.

This is Tunstall Camping Barn, converted and restored by a local farmer with support from the Broads Authority, Broadland District Council, the Ministry of Agriculture and National Westminster Bank.

It offers simple accommodation — similar to camping but without the tent. It consists of a communal sleeping and eating area, somewhere to prepare food (bring your own utensils) and a bathroom area with a loo and hot shower. There is room to sit outside and a paved area for barbecues. It sleeps up to 20; people under 18 must be accompanied by an adult, and dogs are not allowed.

The key is available from Manor Farm, in the centre of Tunstall, and should be collected before 6 pm. Details from the Broads Authority on 0603 610734.

If you do need accommodation, there can hardly be a more inspiring place to greet the morning, since the barn is in the heart of grazing marshes, with little else on the horizon other than sheep and cows.

The route continues to follow the track past the barn through, or round the gate, and goes between two dykes. Take a look in the dykes on the right — they are crystal clear and full of water plants.

At the end of the meadow, climb over the stile, and this leads along a more enclosed section of path until it comes to a crossroads of tracks. Weavers' Way is straight on, but to get to Acle Station turn left. Keep on this track as it turns to road, passing a sewage works (see the *Acle walk*) and industrial estate on the right, and then houses. At the junction, turn right and then take the footpath to the station on the left, just past the woodyard.

Lingwood and Strumpshaw

This walk starts in the village of Lingwood, and heads out through the countryside and passes the front door of Strumpshaw Fen nature reserve, run by the Royal Society for the Protection of Birds. The route dips into the Yare valley, and when it climbs out once again, the views are stunning.

Start	Lingwood Railway Station
Finish	Lingwood Railway Station
⚓	-
👣	7 miles
⌚	2½ hours
🗺	Landranger sheet 134

Buckenham church in 1940. Today the church, with its unusual octagonal tower, is in the care of the Redundant Churches Trust.

LINGWOOD Station is a tourist attraction in itself. On Sunday afternoons in the height of the summer, people out for an afternoon drive will make a special detour to Lingwood to see what has essentially become a public garden. Behind the hanging baskets, the over-flowing tubs of bright annuals, the trailing lobelia and the pungent geraniums is Mrs Joy Long, the crossing keeper, and a group of fellow gardening enthusiasts. They have poured their hearts and souls and a lot of compost into the station gardens to be rewarded with first place in the regional Best Kept Station Award, and a second place in the national competition. It truly is a stunning sight, and even the most hardened commuter on the Norwich to Great Yarmouth line will lower their newspaper to take a look.

Take the only road out of the station, and then turn left into Station Road, passing the King's Head pub. Lingwood is one of those villages that mushroomed almost beyond recognition in the 1970s, with bungalows and estates seemingly growing up overnight. Today the village remains something of a dormitory and commuter belt of Norwich, but it is surrounded by some unbeatable countryside.

At the next junction turn left into Church Road which leads to more open countryside and to St Peter's Church with its huge oak tree dominating the church path. At the end of Church Road, there is a public footpath waymarked to the left which follows the line of a sturdy hedgerow along the edge of a field heading towards a cluster of houses. When the path meets the road turn right and then left at the T-junction, and then next right into Pack Lane. This turns to a track and heads across an open field. It reaches a crossroads of footpaths on a slight rise and from this vantage point there is good view of modern Norfolk countryside — large cultivated fields, oak trees of varying maturity and clipped, machine-cut hedgerows.

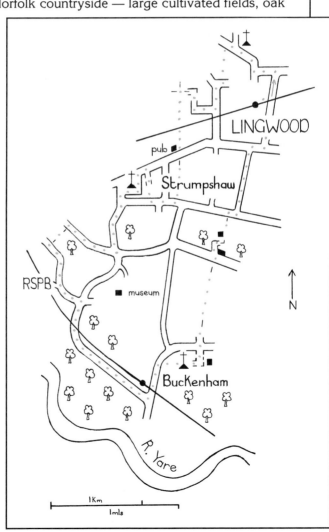

Take the path to the left which quickly turns into a narrow path past a house on the left. Cross the railway line, and the path then becomes enclosed between two hedgerows, sloping down slightly to emerge next to the Huntsman pub and opposite Strumpshaw Post Office.

Cross the road and take the footpath passing the post office and then a house on the right and then continuing uphill between fields. It may be a bit of a slog but it is worth it at the top. Turn round and there is a panoramic view taking in the church, fields, red roofs of Lingwood and the glint of metal as the sun catches the cars speeding along the main Norwich to Great Yarmouth road.

Turn right, passing the riding stables on the left where you might hear the sound of a riding teacher encouraging a young protégé. Opposite the gate to Strumpshaw Riding Centre, (notice the name written in horseshoes) is a footpath leading to the right. This leads past a series of back gardens cluttered with toys, swings, washing and dogs, and humming with lawnmowers. Turn left when the path, which widens to a track, joins the road and then continues past the Shoulder of Mutton pub, and cut through the churchyard of St Peter's Church to Strumpshaw.

It is an unusual church to look at. The tower seems enormous while the body of the church seems low and long. Walk through the churchyard and turn left when you join the road, then an immediate right into Barn Hill. Pause and look across to the skyline of Norwich, a skyline of towers, spires, one or two block buildings, and cranes; indicating the continual development associated with any modern city.

Barn Hill is a shady lane overarched with trees but when you emerge into the sunlight the view is of one looking down on the Yare Valley. Follow the road down hill and at the crossroads turn right. About half a mile further on, just past a bank of trees on the left, is a footpath to the left crossing a meadow until it joins a parallel road. Turn left here and this will lead you past the entrance to Strumpshaw Fen Nature Reserve, owned and managed by the RSPB.

Continue past the reserve to the T-junction. About half a mile along the road, to the left, is the Strumpshaw Steam Museum. Our route takes the road to the right which leads to the railway line. Cross this line and be sure not to miss on the left a tiny white-washed crossing-keeper's cottage teeming with garden gnomes caught in every conceivable act — well almost.

The lane continues with woods on the right and fields on the left. Buckenham church appears on the horizon and to the right are magnificent views leading down to the river Yare.

Continue on the road until reaching Buckenham Railway Station on the left — a sad looking little station, uncared for and in decay. Cross the line (Cantley Sugar Beet Factory can be seen along the line) and continue up the hill with your back to the Yare. As the rise levels out, turn and enjoy the view. If you are lucky the river might be dotted with the white, brown and red sails of small boats striving for the best line. Framed against the wide skies the picture is the epitome of the Broads.

Take the footpath on the right, crossing a field and heading towards Buckenham Church of St Nicholas with its unusual octagonal tower.

This church is no longer in regular use but was declared redundant in 1968 and has since been maintained by the Redundant Churches Trust. When they took it over it was in something of a sorry state. The report by the Redundant Churches Trust confirms this fact by stating that "much of the rendering has fallen away, glass is broken, and the fabric generally is deteriorating".

But this small church, marooned on the north bank of the river Yare, is actually highly unusual. There are a number of early Norfolk towers — just pre-Conquest or Norman — which are round, and a good many were heightened by the addition of an octagonal belfry stage. But Buckenham is thought to be quite exceptional because the tower is octagonal from the base upwards, in other words it was built as an octagonal tower. It also held the distinction of once housing the oldest bell in Norfolk, cast in about 1290. It is thought to have been stolen in July 1973.

Another unusual feature about this sad little church is that it has a dove or pigeon cote in the tower which dates from the 18th century, and such dovecotes in church towers are something of a rarity.

At the track turn left, passing houses and a huge barn with an enormous corrugated-iron roof. Cross over a road and take the path running between two fields. This long path takes you out of the valley, but don't neglect to turn and enjoy the view of the church, the valley, and even Cantley Sugar Beet Factory with its clouds of belching smoke.

At the road turn left and then immediately right onto a track which runs down the left-hand side of a house. At the end of the track is a cottage and the path goes to the right of this cottage. It leads between fields and then joins the road. Turn right, and after about a quarter of a mile turn left along a waymarked footpath which strikes out across a field towards the village of Lingwood. It goes between some houses then comes out in the village. Cross straight over which takes you onto Station Road and then left into the station.

Martham and West Somerton

This is a walk on the wilder side of the Broads. Martham and West Somerton are less popular with tourists, but for those who value unspoilt landscapes, the area is unrivalled. At Somerton church, don't miss the tall story of Robert Hales, the Norfolk giant, who stood nearly 8 feet tall in his stockinged feet.

Start	Martham village centre
Finish	Martham village centre
⚓	-
👣	12 miles
⌚	4½ hours
⏱	Landranger sheet 134

Martham Ferry, across the River Thurne

MARTHAM and West Somerton are in a more remote corner of the Broads which remains still relatively undiscovered by the majority of people holidaying in the area. Potter Heigham Bridge, with its low arch, is a natural barrier for those in cruisers. Although many can negotiate the bridge, it has to be at the right time for the tide and with the aid of the Potter Bridge pilot. Consequently, many never bother, preferring instead the brighter lights associated with Potter Heigham, Wroxham and Horning.

But seek out Martham and you will not be disappointed. It is an altogether wilder area and its nature conservation value cannot be exceeded anywhere in the Broads. Although it is no longer on a train route, buses run regularly there from Great Yarmouth.

When the Romans colonised East Anglia, most of what is now the Broads was a great estuary which the Romans called Gariensis. Within this vast area of sea and mudflats there were several patches of higher ground which formed very bleak islands, for the most part unsettled by both native and Romans alike. During the fifth and sixth centuries, a few Anglo-Saxon settlers eked out an existence by wild-fowling and fishing on these islands, or 'holmes' as they called them. In the following centuries invading Danes settled in East Anglia and, being used to farming marginal land, they had no problem settling in the Martham area. The locality now abounds with Scandinavian place names denoted by the ending 'by', while the name of the whole area 'flegg', is the Danish word for flat.

By the time the Domesday Survey was carried out for William the Conqueror in 1086, there was a thriving sheep farming economy supporting a population two or three times that of West Norfolk.

From the bus stop, walk up Black Street which is behind the bus shelter. Martham church is on the right, and then the road bends to the right, but the route lies left down Staithe Road. This too bends to the right, and after a further mile reaches the end of the boat dyke.

Martham Dyke is delightfully wild and unkempt. Many of the boats moored in it are weathered and worn working boats, some perhaps with a glamourous history, but now sad, sunken wrecks. Go down the right hand bank of the dyke which leads to the river Thurne and to Martham Ferry. For as long as men have been farming the marshes on the Hickling side of the river there has been a ferry at Martham, although 'ferry' is perhaps rather a grand term for a floating pontoon, hauled across the river by hand on a chain.

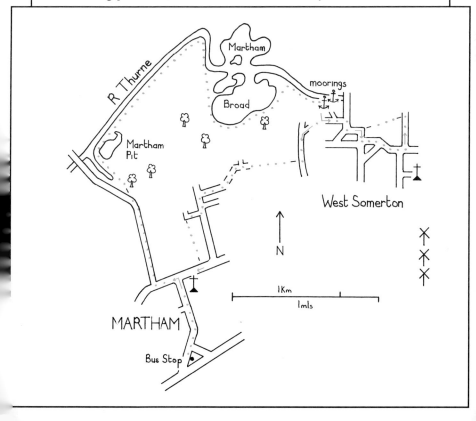

River Thurne at Martham

Broads writer G Christopher Davies encountered the ferry when sailing on the Thurne in the 1880s. He wrote, in his immensely popular book *The Handbook to the Rivers and Broads of Norfolk and Suffolk*: "It is a wonderfully clumsy thing to look at and is not regarded with friendly eyes by the wherrymen, who run their wherries full tilt against it too often at night, or when ... they are unable to stop."

Thankfully no-one behaves in such a cavalier fashion towards the ferry today, which is used mainly for farm traffic. It is still worked manually — farm workers haul on a long chain to get from one side of the river to the other, bringing livestock, tractors, combine harvesters, and vehicles on and off the marshes.

Follow the path along the river's edge to the right. On the right are Martham Pits, today a popular fishing ground, but originally brick pits which were later used as a source of clay for repairing the river walls.

The riverside path is soon hidden from the river by vegetation and in summer is populated by dragon and damsel flies, butterflies and other insects. On the opposite side of the river is the start of Norfolk Naturalists' Trust Reserve which covers 147 acres and includes the two Martham Broads, north and south, as well as reed and sedge beds and alder carr surrounding the open water.

Martham Broads, in common with much of the area known as the Upper Thurne, are some of the most important areas for wildlife in the Broads. The water of these broads is in as near pristine condition as it is possible to get in the Broads, which means an abundance of plants, both in the water and on the fens and grazing marshes. In short, the area is unique in the Broads. Its value lies not so much in the odd rare species which pop up, but in the great diversity of plant and animal life. The whole area, which includes Hickling Broad, Heigham Sound and Horsey Mere, as well as Martham Broad, attracts outstanding numbers of wintering wildfowl — teal, gadwall pochard and goldeneye. In the fringing reed swamp, unparalleled elsewhere in the Broads, are nesting sites for pochard, mallard, tufted duck and shoveler. Reed and sedge beds support nationally important breeding populations such as marsh harrier, bearded tit, cettis and savis warblers. This is also one of the last strongholds of the bittern in the Broads.

The path leaves the bank at a sharp bend in the river and continues through the countryside until it starts to curve to the left and begins to skirt the edge of Martham Broad. The river Thurne flows through the middle of the broad and boats are restricted to the central channel. For once, walkers are more privileged, for the route passes close to the edge of the broad.

The path leading round the broad's edge is wooded and shady, with oaks that have grown twisted and contorted in their efforts to reach the light. From mid-June through July and sometimes into August, the flashing brilliance of the swallowtail butterfly can be seen flying across the paths — a sight which can only be witnessed in the Broads.

ℹ *The unmistakable and distinctive black and yellow colouring of the swallowtail butterfly makes it a beautiful insect and sadly one which has been a target for collectors over the years. Around the turn of the century butterfly collecting was something of a passion for many people. Because of its rarity value and its inimical beauty the swallowtail became a hunted creature and there were plenty of bounty hunters ready for the chase.*

It was said the marshmen and locals in Broadland villages all knew about swallowtails and had a pretty shrewd idea where they could be found, and when. There was a price of about half a crown (12^1/2p) for a caterpillar or a chrysalis.

The chrysalis hatches from about the first of May onwards, with a second hatch of butterflies about the middle of July. The caterpillars abound in August and then turn into their chrysalis form at the end of September ready to hatch out the following spring.

The caterpillars themselves have striking markings yet are not easy to find. They are brown and white, and after about three moults turn into a brilliant apple-green colour banded with purplish velvet-black.

Swallowtails were once to be found all over the country, in particular at Wicken Fen in Cambridgeshire and in Suffolk, but their decline is linked with the change in the landscape. As traditionally managed fens have disappeared so has the rearing ground for the native swallowtail caterpillar's food — the milk parsley.

But even though the plant grew in profusion in the Broads 20 years ago, the insects still took a hammering. The coypus played their part, and persistent flooding across their habitats could well have contributed to destroying many potential butterflies in their chrysalis form.

Thankfully the swallowtail is making something of a comeback. Its presence is by no means widespread all over the area but in certain places — notably Hickling and How Hill — if you take a walk on a warm summer's day you are quite likely to spot one. Just leave your net at home.

A wide belt of trees and undergrowth separates the path from the edge of the open water, but gaps in the vegetation allow precious glimpses of the broad, where doleful cormorants hunch on marker posts. Common terns nest on two specially constructed platforms, and in some years, black terns pass through in spring.

Continue on the path which passes through a gate with a Norfolk Naturalists' Trust notice attached. The path then leaves the enclosed, almost stifling atmosphere of the woodland, and climbs on to the raised flood-bank, exposed to the elements. The views are open once again, with windpumps on the skyline. The path leads to West Somerton Dyke, a wonderfully rural and natural dyke with no shops or modern development, just a few chickens and cockerels strutting about, and a dog barking on a nearby farm.

At the end of the dyke turn right and go through the kissing gate. At this point it is possible to take a detour to Somerton church by turning left after the gate up the Tarmac road. At the T-junction by the Post Office turn right and the road winds through the village. Keep bearing left until it leaves the village, then take the next right by the war memorial, signposted for the church. A sharp left bend brings you face to face with St Mary's — the lovely rural church of Somerton — which is dwarfed by the awesome presence of ten mighty wind turbines, harnessing wind power. This is the only such wind farm in the country and its siting, just outside the official Broads area, was the subject of much controversy. To some, the turbines are an intrusion in the landscape, to others they are an elegant feature and a 'green' way of producing electricity.

Somerton church is also famed for another sort of giant since it is the resting place of Robert Hales the Norfolk giant.

✍ *Robert Hales, the Norfolk giant, was for some people just a marvellous money-spinning freak. To others he was a kindly Norfolk farmer — a gentle giant who would risk his life to save others. Robert was born in Somerton on May 2 1813. In his prime he was 7ft 8ins, weighed 33 stone, and his vital statistics read thus: chest 64 ins, waist 62 ins, thigh 36 ins, calf 21 ins.*

Records stress that he was not a half wit, but a quick-witted intelligent man who rather reluctantly used his massive size to earn a decent living. He inherited his great stature from his mother, one of whose ancestors, a warder in the Tower of London in the reign of Henry VIII, was reputed to have touched 8ft.

Robert's first job was on a trading wherry, but he quickly outgrew the forepeak cabin and went to sea. The same fate again befell him and he outgrew his ship of the line in the Royal Navy and was discharged. With heavy heart he turned to show business, first appearing on Great Yarmouth's Britannia Pier, then in a caravan at Norwich Tombland Fair with his 7ft 3in sister, Mary. She was to share his circus life for three years before dying while on tour in Guernsey.

In 1848 Robert met an agent of the famous showman Phineas T Barnum and was persuaded to try his fortune in America. He went on show alongside a 25 in midget called Tom Thumb. The duo were rapturously received and Barnum arranged a whirlwind tour during which Robert was seen by 28,000 people in 13 days.

But fame and fortune were not his style. He missed England, and despite financial incentives to stay, he returned home when his contract ran out. More fame followed in England. He was presented to Queen Victoria, Prince Albert and six of the royal children.

His last days have a touch of pathos about them. He ended up on the streets of Norwich selling penny leaflets telling the story of his life. Ill-health dogged him towards the end of his days and he died of consumption at the age of 43.

Leave the church and re-trace your steps to the war memorial. Turn right and almost immediately left down a road called The Street. This leads to a small cluster of houses, and just before a brick and flint house is a footpath with a stile hidden in the hedge on the left. Take this raised path, which opens out across fields with views to the right of the sea wall. Go through the cycle barrier at the other side of the field, and continue on the grass track which passes the back of a house and emerges on a road. Turn right and take the second left back into Staithe Road. Fork left at the farm entrance and carry straight on, passing the kissing gate on the right, and running parallel with the dyke.

This weaves and turns until it reaches a road. Turn left, and walk about 100 metres on this road until there is a public footpath signed to the right heading between two fields. This is higher ground, so there are good views to the right across the valley. Stick to the clearly defined path, later turning to a track, and leading towards a group of houses and a stile. Continue on the track which passes houses, track and a former youth hostel all on the left-hand side.

At the T-junction turn left, and then right into Moregrove Lane. Just before the farmyard turn left onto a footpath across a field towards the houses of Martham. At the other side the path turns right along the field edge and almost immediately curves left to the hedge, turning into a grass path going between houses, with walls to the right and tall conifers to the left. Climb over the stile and you reach the road. Turn right and after about 50 metres turn left down Black Street and from there to the church and bus stop.

Reedham

This is a short stroll round Reedham, a popular riverside destination for visitors. Be sure to visit the church, lying slightly out of the village, standing sentinel on the edge of what in Roman times was once a vast estuary.

Start	Reedham Railway Station
Finish	Reedham Railway Station
⚓	Reedham Quay
👣	3 miles
⌚	1 hour
🗺	Landranger sheet 134

Pleasure wherry Hathor *passes Reedham Staithe*

TO stand at Reedham on the banks of the river Yare and look across the marshes is to get an inkling of what it must have been like in Roman times. For then the area was one big estuary called Gariensis, and Reedham was a port. Today there is still that feeling of being on the edge of a country. The village itself is stacked on the north side of the river Yare, and both ends of the village are bordered by crossing points, the swing railway bridge and the chain ferry.

In summer Reedham hums with gentle holiday activity. Postcards are wheeled out to the front of gift shops, and people on cruisers moor up at the quay to buy their ice-creams and feed the ubiquitous ducks. In winter the village appears somnolent, with the stark views across marshes.

On leaving the station car park, turn left up a road called The Havaker, past Reedham Top House, towards the brick-built bridge which straddles the railway line. Turn left over this bridge and follow this road which is taking you away from the village and the river towards the higher ground where the church stands. Look out for the complex of beautifully converted farm buildings to the right, and then turn right onto Church Road. At the next T-junction turn right again, following Church Road, signposted to the marshes.

The church of St John the Baptist is not to be missed. But not for the predictable reasons. Enter this church and it has a curious

Reedham Swing Bridge across the river Yare

lightness and airiness to it, not often found in Norfolk country churches. The walls are whitewashed, the pews are of a light-stained wood, and there is no cumbersome rood screen. The reason for the feeling of otherness about this church was that in 1981, while restoration of the tower was under way, the church was gutted by fire, leaving only the tower and curtain walls.

With 1,300 years of worship on the site behind them, the villagers chose to rebuild their church on the same site, rather than in the village a mile away. As the church guide records: "With prayer, determination and self sacrifice, the villagers rebuilt the church to the Glory of God in just 15 months." It was re-opened by the Bishop of Thetford, the Rt Rev Timothy Dudley-Smith, in June 1982.

The fire revealed the unusual construction of the church walls, made of wrought blocks of freestone interlaid with bricks and flax tiles, undoubtedly of Roman origin, and thought to be part of the Roman Pharos, or lighthouse, which would have stood on the edge of the estuary. The loss of the plaster during the fire revealed the attractive herringbone pattern of brickwork which can be seen both inside and outside the building. The Department of Environment gave a grant towards the restoration on the condition that a piece of the wall structure remained exposed. This has been duly done, near the pulpit.

Leave the church and turn left into Church Dam which leads to a railway crossing. Cross the line and join the footpath which forks to the right and is marked to the village. The path climbs slightly, giving a grand view across the marshes and the river Yare. On a clear day you

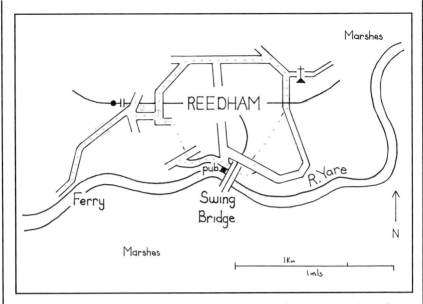

can see Great Yarmouth. The well-trodden path follows the edge of a field on the left, and on the right is a steep railway cutting. It emerges on another impressive three-arched railway bridge. Be sure to cross the road to enjoy a good view of the swing bridge and the marshes.

The swing bridge was opened in 1847 by the Great Eastern Railway Company, carrying the branch line from Reedham to Lowestoft. Today it seems something of an anachronism, a railway bridge which at times must be moved to allow the passage of a boat on the water, but such were the priorities in the Broads. Today, the electrically operated bridge does not regularly have to swing, as few big ships now use the Yare. An exception are the coasters and tankers which journey to Cantley.

Turn left along the road, going away from the village, until you come to a path on the right joining the road at a sharp angle. Go down this path, marked 'unsuitable for motors' and fork right at the bottom, past the back of houses on the left. The path comes out close by the swing bridge itself, and there is a small patch of green grass from where you can marvel closely at the great iron structure.

Continue walking, under the edge of the bridge, coming out near the Ship pub on the left, and public toilets on the right. Join the road and fork left along the village quay.

ℹ *Reedham turned out some of the finest wherries. Hall's Yard was building wherries up until 1906. One of the best known was* **Fawn,** *renowned for her success in wherry races which were a feature of many a regatta. She was a small wherry and not built for carrying cargoes, but won her owner, Isaac Wales, a Reedham timber merchant, many a prize. In his* *fascinating book,* **Wherries and Waterways,** *Robert Malster records how the skipper 'Ophir' Powley used to carry a basket of homing pigeons with him when racing at sea, and would send one home at the end of each round with a message for the vessel's owner waiting at Reedham.*

The Hall family also built the trading wherry **Maud** *in 1900, now being restored at Upton Dyke. Several pleasure wherries also came from Hall's.* **Solace** *was built in 1903 and is still afloat, as is* **Hathor,** *built for the Misses Ethel and Helen Colman, of mustard fame, in 1905.* **Hathor,** *having been fully restored, can still be seen on the Broads, and forms part of the fleet of Wherry Yacht Charter.*

Boatyards still form part of the riverside scene at Reedham, their cranes towering above houses and buildings. Past Sanderson's boatyard, the road veers away from the river and climbs slightly to join a parallel road. Turn right into The Hills, and just past the war memorial on the left is a footpath marked to the station. This takes you into the hinterland away from the river, with the church visible to the right, and Cantley Sugar Beet Factory to the left. The path then follows the edge of a field, at the end of which, turn left walking past terraced houses and bend round to the right before reaching, once again, the first railway bridge you crossed. This time, turn left before you reach the bridge and walk down The Havaker into the station.

However, before you catch your train, there is a detour which should not be missed. Walk straight out of the station, and cross over to join Ferry Road which takes you away from the village towards the marshes. The views are open and vast, with swans, lapwings and other birds grazing on the land, and the distinctive smell of roast sugar beet wafting from Cantley — if the wind is in the right direction.

The road leads towards Reedham Ferry, a chain-link diesel-powered ferry, which until very recently was the only crossing on the Yare between Great Yarmouth and Norwich that was for vehicles. The opening of the Norwich southern bypass has meant the building of a new viaduct across the Yare. The Reedham Ferry takes cars, small trucks, bikes, motorbikes and foot passengers, chugging its way laboriously from side to side, dodging the sailing cruisers in summer, and causing consternation for motor cruisers. The pub offers a warm welcome and good food.

At this point it is possible to walk back in the direction of Reedham along the river, but unfortunately the path is a dead end, with no right of way through a boatyard which would take you into the village. But, if you enjoy riverbank walking, hearing the whispering of reeds, and watching the river traffic sail by, then the short walk along the riverbank and back is worthwhile. The end of the public right of way is clearly marked.

Retrace your steps along Ferry Road to the station.

Salhouse

Retrace the steps of the man credited with discovering the Broads. It was in the 1880s that G Christopher Davies moored at Salhouse and enjoyed a Sunday morning stroll through fields and country lanes to church. This route takes in some of the sights and sounds he may have seen.

Start	Salhouse Railway Station
Finish	Salhouse Railway Station
⚓	Salhouse Broad (small fee)
👣	6 miles
⌚	2 hours
🗺	Landranger sheet 134

Wherries moored at Salhouse Broad

A CLASSIC Victorian Broads writer, G Christopher Davies, once spent a memorable weekend moored in his sailing cruiser on Salhouse Little Broad and wrote about his experiences in *Norfolk Broads and Rivers*.

Early on the Sunday morning, Davies was up and ready for "a leisurely stroll between the lanes, so sweet-smelling and gaily decked with flowers, and over the yellow corn-fields to Salhouse Church".

This walk follows a similar route and many of the sights, sounds and smells Davies recorded are still there to be appreciated over 100 years later. Salhouse is one of the few Broads villages with good access for walkers to the open water of a broad. So often broads are enclosed by trees and scrub, or can only be tantalisingly viewed from a tiny public staithe. But Salhouse is different.

Starting from the railway station, head for the road and turn left under the railway bridge. Continue along this road until you come to Howlett's Loke on the left. Turn down this lane (not the public footpath, that's on the way back).

The lane opens out, with fields on the right, and the station to the left. The route runs parallel with the railway line, dipping slightly and taking a slight kink. The path then continues close to the line, separated from it by a thick jungle of brambles, gorse and ferns. The church can be glimpsed to the right.

Where the footpath crosses the railway line, your route takes you to the right, not along the private drive, but along the clearly demarcated footpath, overarched with trees, passing Redwings Farm on the left. At the end of this section the path is waymarked Norfolk County Council Circular Walk. The path curls to the left, passing a bank of woodland on the left, with big views across agricultural land elsewhere.

At the end of the wood, the walking is exposed, bisecting two huge agricultural fields, tailor-made for big farm machinery, but farmed by someone not too big to forget the little things in life like public footpaths.

The path hits the main road, which our route takes us across, then along the track to the right of Salhouse church where Davies attended a Sunday morning service back in the 1880s.

In many ways, Davies is the man credited with discovering the Broads and subsequently writing about them. "There is no better 'playground' in England, and certainly none easier of access or more cheaply to be enjoyed than the Broad District," he wrote... "with the aid of a small yacht, short intervals of rest can be employed in the most agreeable manner, and with the minimum of expenditure". In many ways, like others of his times, he romanticised the area, but nevertheless had a genuine love for it. He described the area as a district "for the most part as flat as a billiard table, where water and land strive for the mastery, and come to a delightful compromise".

The track turns into a footpath opening out with a hedge on the right and a field to the left. Continue straight until the path joins the road. Turn right and head towards the village houses, noting the duck pond on the right. Old thatch and new red brick blend surprisingly well. The architecture is never predictable, the gardens are different shapes and sizes, making it a lively and interesting discovery route.

The road dips, and at the junction where there is a small village green, turn left and walk about 50 metres towards a small car park for Salhouse Broad. Just before you reach it, don't miss the bundles of reed stacked outside the home of a thatcher.

i *Norfolk reed (Phragmites communis) is not actually confined to Norfolk, but also grows in Suffolk, Kent, Essex, Dorset, Hampshire and Glamorgan. It is known as the Prince of Thatch, and is thought to be the best money can buy for thatching, lasting at least 70 years.*

The reed in the Broads is harvested in the cruelest months, from December through to March. In the past, the marshman would cut it by hand with rhythmical strokes of a scythe.

Norfolk Reed, known as the Prince of Thatch. This reed is being harvested on the Broads Authority's reserve at How Hill

Today machinery has been brought in which cuts and loosely ties the reed into bundles. Broads naturalist Ted Ellis once wrote in his regular Eastern Daily Press column that reed cutting is a tough job. "Reeds are so abrasive that they even wear down the finger nails of those who handle them regularly. They also reduce jackets to tatters very quickly through the carrying of bundles. If a wind is blowing while cutting is in progress reed plumes have a habit of striking the face and eyes, causing much discomfort. Splintering stalks cut the hands inevitably every day."

The demand for Norfolk reed is high. The Broads Authority, which has reed beds on its nature reserve at How Hill, Ludham, could sell the reed many times over. The same goes for the Norfolk Naturalists' Trust at Hickling.

The walk leading from the car park to Salhouse Broad takes about ten minutes. If you visit in winter — probably the best time — then the noise of the broad reaches you before the sight of it. Flocks of greylag, Canada geese and ducks congregate here, barracking and brawling as they fly in to land. The geese are actually something of a sore point in the Broads. Their numbers have increased in recent years, and whereas they used to be found mainly on Salhouse and Wroxham Broads, they are now more widespread. They are highly unpopular with many boat owners who have to clear up their droppings from the boat decks. But to many holidaymakers they are part of the wildlife scene.

ℹ️ *In the early days of sailing on the Broads, Victorians and Edwardians treated the experience as something of an adventure, but an adventure which nevertheless was comfortably padded at the edges. The novelty of such holidays is illustrated by a book written in 1897 by E R Suffling called* How to Organise a Cruise on the Broads. *Clearly the author thought people needed a step by step guide, and in many ways they did, since the hire fleets were in their infancy.*

Wherries were clearly the top-of-the-range craft, equipped in some cases with a yacht piano. By this time, the wherry builders had diversified and craft were built especially for holiday parties — 'pleasure wherries' and 'wherry yachts' as they were known. The cost would have been about £10 – £12 a week in July and August, dropping to £8 – £9 for the low season. Next down the list came what Suffling described as an 'ordinary' 12 ton yacht, accommodating two ladies and four gentlemen, with a man and lad working the vessel and sleeping and cooking in the peak — the tiny cabin at the front.

Suffling also includes a mighty list of provisions to take — enough to feed a family for a month. It includes beef, pork, fowl, duck, ox tongue, rabbit, flour, cheese, sardines, dried haddocks, tinned fruit, fresh fruit, mustard, vinegar, pepper, Worcester sauce, pickles, bread, biscuits — plain and fancy — and beer, spirits and wine, all according to tastes. But he does not stop there. He goes on to tell them what to pack in their cases, including one pair of India-rubber-soled tennis shoes, flannel trousers, shirts, blazer and cap, travelling rug, shaving tackle, two or three books for a wet day, and smoking apparatus.

But what really takes the biscuit (plain or fancy) is his advice about keeping warm at night. Feet, he says, may be thrust into the sleeves of a coat, the body of which is then rolled round the legs and feet. But those scared of draughts should have recourse. In his book Suffling tells them, to the

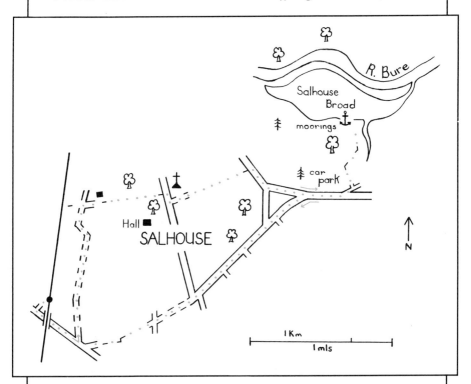

"Crimean nightcap, such as our soldiers made for themselves with a pocket handkerchief during the Russian War in 1854 – 6".

It is from Salhouse Broad that the Broads Authority has in past years run summer boat trips, on board a quiet pollution-free launch, to visit Hoveton Great Broad nature trail, which forms part of the Bure Marshes National Nature Reserve. Passengers disembark at the broad and walk round a trail laid out by English Nature, and pass through wonderful swamp carr, alder woodland and fen. The trip is memorable, and it is worth phoning to see if a boat is running and timing your trip accordingly.

Leaving the broad, retrace your steps along the path to the car park and turn right back towards the village. Continue straight past the village green, along Lower Street, a street lined with houses, cottages, modern chalet bungalows, and tucked away on the left a tiny village hall, erected in 1897 in commemoration of 60 years reign of Queen Victoria. The road also passes Salhouse Equestrian Centre.

Lower Street comes to an end at a T-junction. Our route lies straight across the junction up a track, marked as a public footpath to Salhouse Station. At the end of the houses the path opens out with a field to the left, and Salhouse Hall can be glimpsed through the trees to the right. The route goes down the side of the field, and there is a kink in the path before it ends at shoulder-high iron bars. The path brings you back to the road. Turn right and retrace your steps under the railway bridge and turn right into the station again.

Sheringham and Beeston Regis

Walking boots at the ready, this walk takes in the second highest point in Norfolk, but don't get too excited, it is only 100m high. The route follows the famous Cromer Ridge, before turning inland to explore an area of National Trust heathland.

Start	Sheringham Railway Station
Finish	Sheringham Railway Station
⚓	-
👣	6 miles
🕐	2 hours
🗺	Landranger sheet 133

Some of the Shannocks of Sheringham, pictured in 1901

> There dwelt beside the great North Sea
> A hale and hearty company
> Of men and women brave and free
> Who called themselves the Shannocks.
> *'The Folk Called Shannocks'*

THE people of Sheringham have come to be known as Shannocks. No one is totally sure of the origin of the word but one well-known Norfolk historian, Walter Rye, said it was derived from a word meaning a wild and reckless lot of people.

Walk down Sheringham's main street today, and no one seems particularly wild or reckless, but turn the clock back a couple of hundred years and witness the daily battle the town's fishermen held with the sea, then perhaps their reputation is justified.

Today Sheringham relies heavily on the holiday industry for its economic stability. In the past, the harvest of the sea was the principal industry, with over 200 boats working at the peak. Now a remnant remains with only a handful of fishermen still bringing in the catches of crabs, lobsters, cod and long-shore herring.

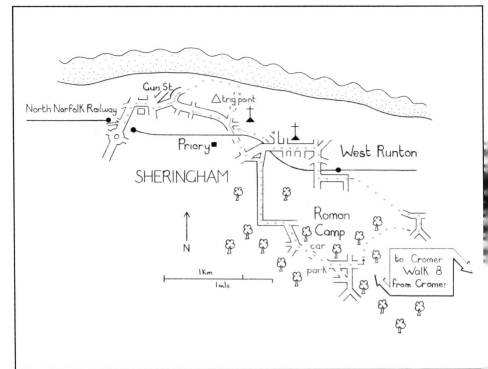

Walk out of the station; ahead is the North Norfolk Steam Railway and a car park with a hectic Saturday market. Turn right down the main street (Station Road) which heads towards the sea, threading through the crowds if it is summer, and locals if winter. Sheringham Museum is located on the left side of Station Road. It is an independently run museum, sited in three former one-up, one-down fishermen's cottages, which were subsequently used as wash houses and net lofts.

Continue walking through the main Sheringham shopping street, characterised by its small, narrow buildings in keeping with the narrow streets. It sends a shudder down any sensitive soul's spine to think that in the 1950s there was a revolutionary plan for Sheringham which envisaged the 'reconstruction' of much of this area. The heart of the town, including the Clock Tower (now restored) was to be pulled down and replaced by a combination which included shops, boarding and apartment houses, conference hall, theatre, winter gardens, offices, hotel, library, art gallery and covered swimming pool. Thankfully in 1975, Sheringham Town Council committed itself to town centre preservation.

Nearing the sea the buildings have appropriately quaint names — Starboard Cottage, Marine Cottage, Two Lifeboats Hotel. The beach at present is pebbly and can seem hostile and wild, but inspiring, in the middle of winter when the waves crash onto the shore, sending jets of spray up the seawall. After this glimpse of the sea, retrace your steps a few yards to Gun Street where there is, not surprisingly, a gun.

The fear of invasion has always been at the back of Sheringham's mind. This is in part because of its proximity to Weyborne Hope, a place of deep anchorage, where it was always thought an enemy could strike. There is a rhyme which goes: "He who would old England win, must at Weybourne Hope begin." In 1588 the threat was from the Spanish Armada. Strict instructions were handed down by military experts that cliffs at Cromer and Sheringham should be slopingly cut; a passage to the water's edge should be blocked up and a parapet built on the top. Trenches were also to be dug on Sheringham Heath — something which was repeated in the First World War. Later, in the reign of Charles I, the country was embroiled with war again and a 'scorched earth' policy was suggested for Sheringham. If the enemy landed, corn would be burnt, cattle driven away, butter, cheese and other food moved to safety along with other valuable household goods and implements.

But a sad state of affairs revealed itself in 1673 when the people of Sheringham pleaded, almost implored, the county for help defending themselves against Dutch pirates, as recounted in A History of Sherringham and Beeston Regis *by A Campbell Errol: ..."we are afraid every night ye enemy should come ashore and fire our Towne when we be in our beds; for ye houses stand very close together, and all ye houses Thatched with straw, that in one houres time ye town may be burnt". And their defence? ..."we have nothing to Resist them But one Gun with a broken carriage and four Musquetts which we bought at our owne cost and charges". The agony continues that they do not even have any powder for "ye said Gun".*

Six muskets with 50 pounds of powder and 50 pounds of bullets were duly dispatched with a warning that the equipment was only to be used in the defence of Sheringham and not embezzled. But 23 years later another six muskets had to be sent to save Sheringham from the 'insults' of French privateers. An official was charged to deliver these arms into the custody of some "honest and discreet inhabitants", and at the same time find out what happened to the other arms and ammunition!

The gun standing at the top of Gun Street could be the very broken down weapon, or could date from plans to protect the coast from the Spanish Armada threat.

Take the next left into Wyndham Street, where on the right is Whitehall Yard which has earned its place in local history through being the recipient of the first bomb to be dropped in The First World War. The incendiary bomb fell from a Zeppelin L.4 on January 19 1915, but did little damage.

Keep left and fork into Cliff Road, a residential street heading uphill towards the cliff tops. The road peters out and turns into a cliff path heading towards Beeston Hill. A quick, fairly steep climb, and the view behind you to the town is enlightening. There, Sheringham can be seen nestling in a hollow between two steep cliff edges. Keep climbing and you reach a trig point.

The walk now follows the route of what is known as the Cromer Ridge, terminal moraine deposited during the last ice age.

What should be a magnificent vista along the ridge towards Cromer is sadly marred by the presence of a caravan site with its box-shaped mobile holiday homes quite out of keeping with the wild open landscape above the sea. After this bracing stretch along the ridge, the route now lies inland. Turn right at the entrance to the caravan park following the path between two fields. Cross the railway line and continue down the track.

On the right are the remains, unfortunately all but hidden from this angle, of Beeston priory. The village was on the pilgrimage route to Walsingham and the priory is thought to have been established in 1197. Like so many small priories it had a turbulent history, culminating when the abbots were accused of committing "manifest sins" and of indulging in "vicious carnal and abominable living". Under Henry VIII it was dissolved in 1539, but its remains today give an idea of its importance, particularly when it came to providing hospitality for travellers.

The track ends at the main road. Cross over and turn left, forking right along another track waymarked as the coastal footpath. Turn right again to lead past Hall Farm on the left and then Beeston Regis Hall. The track climbs towards a woodland, passing between two fields until it reaches Beeston Regis Heath. Turn left and follow the edge of the wood; after about 50 metres a yellow long-distance footpath arrow points to a path forking right along the edge of a small pine plantation.

Keep the fence and woodland on the right, ignoring any footpaths leading off to the left. The path then bends right and heads up into the wood and you are soon walking up through a gully carving a way into an enchanting woodland.

𝓲 *At Beeston Regis Heath the National Trust has undertaken a plan to clear invading scrub and trees and restore the typical heathland habitat. In February 1992 the Trust embarked on work to clear 200 pine, birch and young oak trees in order to link two surviving areas of heathland and to control further invasion of trees on the fringes of the heath.*

Heathland is a traditional habitat once grazed by sheep which weeded out invasive plants like bracken, birch and pine trees. Local people would also have gathered bracken for cattle bedding, and heather for thatching. Grazing at West Runton stopped in the early years of the 20th century and ever since, without a regular management regime, the open heathland areas have declined.

The Trust was spurred into action after it was asked to take part in a national survey to see just how much heathland remained. Staff were astonished to find the amount of heathland at West Runton had dropped from eight to five acres in a matter of years.

Once cleared, the task of keeping it clear should not prove too onerous, being a matter of stopping tree saplings from becoming established. Until the 1950s rabbits would have done this task for nothing, but the outbreak of myxomatosis decimated the rabbit population and gave saplings a chance to get a hold.

Nationally, heathlands are fast disappearing from the landscape as a result of intensive farming, tree planting and building development. But it is a habitat well worth preserving, being home to birds like the nightjar and stonechat, as well to butterflies, lizards and snakes.

It is possible to explore the surrounding woodland from the National Trust car park. There is a myriad of paths which are regularly walked by locals who know their way about. For anyone with a poor sense of direction, a compass might be helpful, as it is easy to get disorientated — we certainly did!

The route continues straight ahead from the wooded gully, passing through the car park and along the track used by cars visiting the area. A little way along on the left is a clearing with a glorious view across to the cliffs and beyond to the sea; a seat means walkers can enjoy the landscape and picnic at the same time. The track continues past a caravan park on the right and comes out in another car park. This area is called Roman Camp, although there was never a Roman camp on the site. Its fame today continues because it is situated next to Beacon Hill, the second highest point in Norfolk — a fact not difficult to achieve. The heathland area around the camp is dotted with shallow circular iron-working pits dating from about 850 to 1100.

Continue on the track, take the left fork, which comes out at a road. Cross over following the coastal footpath sign and turn left, ignoring the ordinary public footpath which goes straight on. This gravel path unfurls down hill surrounded on either side by trees, but gradually massive rhododendrons become more prominent, until further on they are growing across the path, shading out the light, just as they shade out the woodland floor, stifling other plants.

The track emerges from the woodland and narrows, entering more open countryside. At a junction in footpaths, continue straight on, passing to the right of a scrubby knoll, following the long distance sign and the Norfolk Heritage Coast sign. The path is more

A view as taken from Roman Camp in 1926. Close by is Beacon Hill, the second highest point in Norfolk.

enclosed now and goes through a kissing gate and continues along the right hand side of a field. It crosses a small stream and carries on through an area of scrub to join a track. Turn left at this point and the route goes towards the village of East Runton.

Our route lies to the left, along a public footpath at the crown of the bend in the road. It follows the line of a flint wall and although it starts off overgrown it comes out into the open with fields on the left and right. Somehow there is a sense that the sea is just over the horizon, and before long it appears. The path skirts to the left round the base of Incleborough Hill with the golf course on the right, and runs close to the railway.

The path ends at a road leading through the golf course. Turn right and this runs parallel with the railway on the right and then the golf course appears on the left. The trackway meets a road leading into the village of West Runton. Opposite is the delightfully wild common where ponies graze. To the left is the Links Hotel with its distinctive turrets which are a trademark of the North Norfolk coast. By turning left at this point you can reach the West Runton Stables where the Norfolk Shirehorse Centre is found. Here they stage working demonstrations of shire horses.

Our route lies to the right, over the railway bridge and into the village of West Runton, from where it is possible to catch a train. The village is unusual in that it is actually one village divided into two — East and West — although its single identity has become clouded over recent years. The village noticed a big change when the railway was built, increasing holiday trade as Runton acted as a kind of over-flow for Cromer and Sheringham. Camping and caravanning became popular during the wars and sites were set up on the cliffs. In the early days the caravans were taken away in the winter months to allow grazing of animals, but that tradition has now ended.

Bear left joining the main road through the village, past Holy Trinity Church. Just before the road crosses the railway bridge, there is a footpath passing to the right of the bridge, marked Footpath to Sheringham. It follows the railway line, past the backs of houses and passes in front of Beeston Regis church.

The path carries on to the level crossing which we crossed earlier in the walk. At this point there is a choice. It is possible to retrace your steps along the cliff edge, or to fork off left up a slight hill towards houses. If you go this way, there is a better view of the priory to the left. The road then goes through a built-up area and joins Cliff Road. At the bottom turn left and then immediate right into Co-operative Street which emerges in the main street once again. Turn left for the station.

Kelling Heath and Weybourne

All aboard the North Norfolk Steam Railway for this walk taking in the wild seashore at Weybourne, and the sultry heathland of Kelling Heath.

Start	Kelling Heath or Weybourne on the North Norfolk Steam Railway
Finish	as start
⚓	-
👣	6 miles
⌚	2 hours
🗺	Landranger sheet 133

Weybourne from Kelling Heath

THE North Norfolk Steam Railway runs over five miles between Sheringham and Holt, passing through some of North Norfolk's most spectacular scenery. Not only is the journey a nostalgic trip back to the days of steam, but its halts at Kelling Heath and Weybourne make it an excellent starting point from which to explore the coast.

ℹ The 'Muddle and Get Nowhere' railway was the nickname adopted by locals for the Midland and Great Northern Joint Railway. The line between Holt, Sheringham and Cromer was opened on June 16 1887. It was built and originally operated by the Eastern and Midlands Railway, completing the branch from Melton Constable to the North Norfolk coast. Later this company merged with others to form the Midland and Great Northern, which subsequently operated the line.

Melton Constable, the start of the branch line to Cromer, was a small sleepy hamlet until the railway came. In the heart of North Norfolk a large works was built with offices and workshops to build and maintain rolling stock and locomotives. Not surprisingly it became known as the 'Crewe of Norfolk'. Houses and schools were built for railway workers; a gas works, sewerage works and bowling green were

Nº 3809 pulls out of Weybourne Station on the North Norfolk Steam Railway. The line passes through some spectacular countryside.

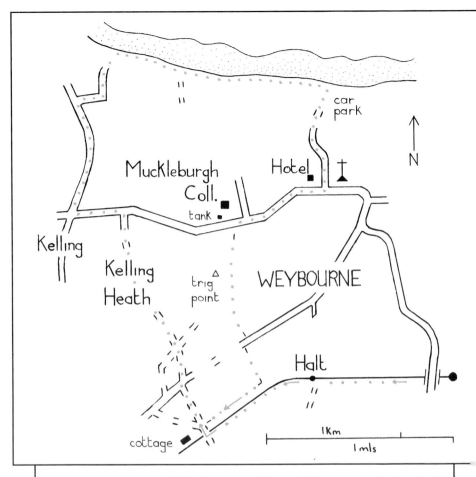

also provided, and in the next village, Briston, a mission hall was built to preach to workers of the evils of the demon drink.

There is a delightful story of a Norfolk mother whose son was about to emigrate to Australia. The local Rector visited her to counsel her about her son's departure and to ensure the old girl knew exactly how far Australia was away from Norfolk. With a sense of awe, she told the clergyman: "I know he's got to change at Melton Constable." It is a story that says a lot about the importance of Melton Constable, but speaks volumes about country life in Norfolk!

The North Norfolk line, or the Poppy Line as it was known, carried thousands of passengers from the Midlands to the coastal holiday towns. Its end came in 1964, when having escaped the Beeching cuts, the line from Melton Constable to Sheringham was closed. The only vestiges left of the glorious M & G N was five miles of line from Sheringham to Cromer operated by British Rail.

But as soon as the closure was mooted, a preservation society was formed which aimed to buy a section of the line and operate steam trains for the public. Originally the society wanted to buy some 20 miles of track, but common sense prevailed and a more manageable three miles between Sheringham and Holt was earmarked.

A company was formed to run the line, the North Norfolk Railway Company, and raised £14,000 when it went public. At the start only members of the society or shareholders were allowed to travel because the company did not have a Light Railway Order — a licence to carry the public: this licence was granted in 1975.

Another major landmark was in 1987 when the second section was opened from Weybourne to Holt, exactly 100 years after it was first opened. It had taken 10 years to restore the section, clearing undergrowth from the track bed and laying the rail, as well as building a new station at Holt.

The railway is run through the dedication of a band of volunteers who continue to drive the trains, man the stations, and maintain and restore the locomotives, buildings and rolling stock.

The walk described here starts at Kelling Heath Park, which is a halt on the line. However, because of the gradient which is 1 in 80, steam trains cannot stop here on their journey up to Holt. Diesel railbus trains do call at the platform in both directions. Alternatively you can stop at Weybourne station and take the footpath which links up with the Kelling Heath Nature Trail, and then Kelling Heath halt.

At Kelling Heath halt, with your back to the sea, turn right and follow the line until you reach a level crossing. Cross here, passing a keeper's cottage on the left, and head across the heath towards the sea. The whole of Kelling Heath is a fascinating complex of heath, woodland, a former gravel pit and pond. The land south of the railway is owned by the company which runs the Kelling Heath Caravan Park. The common land to the north is administered by a board of trustees.

In the late 1980s North Norfolk District Council approached the owners of the caravan park to see if

Kelling Heath, a fascinating complex of heath, woodland and water

they would consider improving public access to the site and carrying out some conservation work. With help from the Countryside Commission, labour from the Manpower Services Commission and materials from the caravan park, a magnificent nature trail has been created and it is a fine example of what can be achieved between the public and the private sector.

The nature trail is marked by squirrel waymarkers and arrows. A number of nesting boxes and bat boxes have been put up around the nature trail, and activity around these is at its peak during the breeding season from March to July. Leaflets about the trail are available from

Farming countryside as viewed from Kelling Heath

stations at Weybourne and Sheringham.

Continue on the track across the heath; cross the road and take the track straight opposite, again through heathland, bordered by head-high gorse. This comes to a large crossroads in the tracks. Ahead lies a sandy area, like a plateau, where cars park; our path lies straight ahead and slightly to the left, not the main track to the left, but a very narrow path through the gorse which leads down through a gully, with higher ground to either side. Be careful, this is an easy one to miss. At the outset this path is enclosed with gorse, but as it descends the heathland ends and the path is bordered by trees and fields.

The trees and hedges immediately give way to the sound of chattering hedgerow birds — something which has been eerily absent from the remote heathland. The path, which turns to a track, comes out on a road. In front is a field, but you can sense the sea beyond.

Turn left along the busy main road until reaching the village of Kelling, and turn right along a track going in front of a group of flint cottages. The track is marked as a public footpath and as being unsuitable for motors. As the path progresses the contrast from the dry sandy heathland is immediately obvious. This is low and wet, and on the right is a reserve called the Quags, bought by the Norfolk Ornithologists Association in 1984. This Association was set up in 1970 to act as a parent body to the Holme Bird Observatory Reserve further west along the coast near Hunstanton. This, in turn, was set up in 1962 in seven acres of pine and scrub-covered dunes near the shore. It is rather like an immigration point for birds. Every day a study of migrating birds is carried out. The numbers present are recorded, while the flight direction of those passing through is also noted.

This path passes the top end of the Quags and then turns to the left to head towards the high shingle bank. You might be mistaken for thinking the roaring sound is that of distant lorries; but it is, of course, the roaring of the waves crashing onto the shingle beach. It is a wild, sometimes hostile beach, often windswept and deserted. The coastal path continues to the right, passing a military installation, and several pill boxes — signs of the strategic importance of this stretch of coastline during the Second World War.

The path reaches Weybourne beach car park and here turns right along the road leading to the village. On reaching the village turn right at the junction, past the village sign, and walk out of the village slightly uphill. Just as the hill begins to flatten out, there is the Muckleburgh Collection on the right. This remarkable collection is now the largest private collection of its kind in the United Kingdom. There has been a military establishment or presence on this stretch of the North Norfolk coast since 1588 in the days of the Spanish Armada, when it was found that the deep water approach afforded a potential invasion landing for enemy forces. Such was the case in the Second World War when the entire coast was protected with mines, anti-tank devices and barbed wire.

🗓 *The Muckleburgh Collection, a military museum, is on the site of a former army camp. A few years before the Second World War it was established as a heavy anti-aircraft temporary training site, with all personnel in tents. These were replaced by prefabricated huts after gales in the winter of 1936/7 blew most of the tentage into the North Sea. The gunners were joined by the RAF who maintained the radio controlled Tiger Moth targets, while ATS and WAAF girls manned the Predictors and Range-finders.*

After the war the camp became the Anti-Aircraft Permanent Range and Radar Training Wing, providing training for national servicemen. The last gun fired on October 1958 and the camp closed in March the following year. The future of the camp was the subject of much deliberation. Options ranged from a marina and holiday camp to oil refinery, prison, or nuclear power station, although Norfolk County Council maintained all along that it should be returned to agricultural use, which is in fact what happened.

However, the original NAAFI building was retained and now houses the Muckleburgh Collection which is dedicated to the men and women who served on the site in all theatres of war. The collection has been assembled by the founders of the Combined Operations Museum at Inverary in Scotland. It was opened to the public in 1988 and with its collection of tanks, armoured cars, artillery and military artefacts, has attracted thousands of visitors. Some of the vehicles have come from many miles — including Canada, Holland, France, the Falkland Islands, the Golan Heights, Vietnam, and from what was behind the Iron Curtain.

The route we have to take is on the opposite side of the road and is unmarked. It is a narrow path leading through the undergrowth about 10 metres from the entrance to the Muckleburgh Collection. The barrel of a tank parked outside the collection points virtually to the path — but beware this tank might now have its sights trained on another target!

The path is well trodden and goes through a small copse. Keep to the left hand edge; the higher you climb through here the better the views across the sweeping fields, woods, the windmill, the village of Weybourne and to the sea. There reaches a point where the trees thin out slightly and there is more bracken and ferns. Here the path splits, the left fork going slightly downhill and the right fork climbing steeply. Take this right fork for a detour to a magnificent view. It goes up between two hillocks and on top of the right hand hillock is a trig point.

Retrace your steps to where the paths split and continue on the left fork which skirts the edge of the wood, with its birdsong and rustling of leaves and creak of timbers. To the left are huge agricultural fields, patterned by straight hedges. The wooded path emerges on a road. Turn right and a further 10 metres on the left is another unmarked path skirting a field to the left and trees and undergrowth to the right. Continue along here until you reach the railway line, turn right up a sandy bank and follow the line back to the keeper's cottage. Cross the line, and turn left along the track re-tracing your steps to Kelling Heath halt, or Weybourne.

Wroxham and Coltishall

Wroxham is the undisputed gateway to the Broads, and it was here that the Broads boating holiday began over a century ago. The walk explores the teeming holiday centres of Wroxham and Hoveton and then moves up river to the pastoral peace of Coltishall and Belaugh.

Start	Wroxham Railway Station
Finish	Wroxham Railway Station
	Coltishall Green or Hoveton Horseshoes, next to Broads Authority Information Centre
	8 miles
	3 hours
	Landranger sheet 134

Surveying the boating scene at Wroxham Bridge on the river Bure

NO book about the Broads would be complete without some reference to Wroxham. In many ways it was here that it all began. When the railways came to Norfolk in the 1860s, Wroxham became the starting point for thousands of Broads holidaymakers.

To be accurate, much of what is taken for Wroxham is in fact Hoveton. The dividing line between the two villages is the river Bure, but poor old Hoveton lost out when the railway from Norwich to Cromer was being planned in the late 1880s. The station planned for Wroxham was moved about a mile up the line towards Cromer — its present site — but the name plates were made with Wroxham on them and they were used even though the station was now in Hoveton.

Today Wroxham (and Hoveton) is a rather gaudy place in high summer. Sprawling development has been allowed to spoil the riverside and huge brick-built homes loom over the water's edge.

For many people Wroxham is synonymous with Roys which used to advertise itself as the 'World's largest village store'. The story of Roys is one worthy of an entrepreneur like Richard Branson. Towards the end of the 19th century, young

Arnold Roy of Wroxham was hawking oranges round the countryside with a donkey (named William) and barrow. At 15 years of age he went to work for a drapery firm in Norwich, sweeping floors and running errands. The metropolis beckoned and at 16 he was working for a shilling a day as a warehouse boy in London, supplementing his income with coppers earned by holding horses' heads and opening cab doors. Later he served an apprenticeship with established retail houses in Norwich and London, returning at 18 to join his brother, Alfred, and sister to run a small shop in Coltishall, bought for them by their father.

The Roys recognised that Wroxham was to be the gateway to the Broads. Many yachts were getting provisions from London, but Alfred and Arnold had other ideas. Alfred bought a shop and Arnold came over to manage it. Yachting people were told to order their groceries and offered a refund on any perishables they did not use; delivery vans were bought to serve the outlying districts; saloon cars were put at the disposal of all distant customers to enable them to shop at the Roys stores.

There was also service to the wider community; the Roys provided street lighting for the village, public toilets, car parking, and litter bins — all, of course, with the Roys name boldly printed on them.

Expansion meant that the Roys now stretched throughout the village — grocery, provisions, drapery, boots and shoes, pharmacy, ironmongery, greengrocer's, tailor's, bakery, fish, fishing tackle, wines, a garage — almost everything was available, and the customers flocked in. In the 1930s they were serving approximately 200,000 customers and had a fleet of 50 delivery vans, and orders valued at £3,000 a week.

Today Roys remains a family concern. The family trading style lives on, and the customers continue to throng in.

On alighting from the train at Wroxham and Hoveton, follow the signs for the Bure Valley Railway, over the footbridge towards the narrow gauge railway station. The route along the Bure Valley Railway Walk is clearly signposted and follows the narrow gauge route, climbing slightly out of the village before levelling off to give uninterrupted views across the surrounding farmland.

No directions are really necessary; you will pass several access points, but your route continues along the walk until you reach the Coltishall halt.

ℹ *The Bure Valley Walk follows part of the route of the former Great Eastern Railway line running between Wroxham and Aylsham, a distance of about nine miles. There are halts on the route at Coltishall, Buxton, and Brampton, allowing walkers to let the train take the strain for part of the route.*

The railway itself had a relatively short working life as a passenger line. Work started in 1878, the contract being awarded at a price of £43,971. Contractor William Waddell employed 187 men, 22 horses and 46 wagons, and despite bad weather and a shortage of manpower, the line was finished ten days before the promised completion date, and opened for freight and passengers on January 1 1880. It was not a success. In the 1880s, typical trains had anything between four and 25 passengers on board. A higher figure was achieved on a Saturday afternoon market train returning from Norwich when there were, sometimes 47 passengers.

Buses proved the next nail in the coffin. The first 'boneshaker' bus started to run from Norwich to Aylsham and Cromer in 1919 and was soon found to be more efficient than the trains. There was a temporary revival in rail traffic as a result of the Second World War when RAF stations at Salhouse, Coltishall and Foulsham generated more passengers and bus schedules were cut. But when the war was over, there was a rapid decline in train passengers, and in 1952 the service closed to passengers. The closure did not go unnoticed. At Buxton the union flag flew at half mast, and in Aylsham the station was decorated with black and white crepe and Chopin's Funeral March was played.

When the last train stopped, detonators were exploded and the driver and fireman were presented with cigars and bottled beer. A dahlia wreath was hung on the engine and the card read: "To the memory of another limb of private enterprise which as amputated during the scourge of nationalisation. 1881-1952." The line remained open to freight until 1982, when it was finally closed to all traffic.

The Bure Valley Railway rose from the ashes when Broadland District Council acquired the track bed from Aylsham to Hoveton. The Bure Valley Railway Company set about the task of constructing a 15 inch gauge steam railway, with new stations being built at Aylsham and Hoveton, and halts at Coltishall, Brampton and Buxton. The project cost about £2.5 million and was opened in July 1990.

By now you have probably reached Coltishall, the end of the line for this walk. Turn left off the path onto the road leading from the former station buildings. Turn right along the main road towards the village, passing the Railway pub on the left and Hautbois Road on the right.

For many who are unfamiliar with the area, Coltishall is associated with RAF Coltishall, home of the Jaguar fighter aircraft. A far cry from the days 150 years ago when the name of Coltishall was synonymous with a very different kind of craft — the wherry, but more of that when we reach the river.

Coltishall Common, tranquil in winter, bustling in summer

In the centre of the village stands a garage on a kind of island at a cross-roads. Turn right here and cross the bridge. Just over the bridge, there is a footpath on the left which follows the river. This ends at the ruins of Horsted Mill, once a working mill producing flour for the local bakeries, but it was burnt down one night in 1963 and has remained a ruin ever since. Unfortunately it is not possible to cross the river at this point, but it does give a good view of Coltishall Upper Common, where once the Whit Monday Fair was held. Today it is maintained admirably by the Coltishall Commons Trust.

Retrace your steps, noting on the right hand bank the remains of the old lock which today marks the limit of navigation on the Bure. A hundred years ago this part of the river Bure would have been a hectic commercial waterway with wherries queuing up at the lock waiting to take their cargoes to Aylsham, probably quanting most of the way.

On reaching the road, turn right across the bridge. This bridge was washed away in August 1912 in some of the fiercest flooding recorded in the Broads. After two days of torrential rain the Bure burst its banks; the bridge was washed away and water flooded into several homes in Horstead and Coltishall. The new bridge was built in 1913. Bear right with the garage on the left, and the common on the right. Take the road running parallel with the river, but not in sight of it, passing the parish church on the right, village shops, and finally the Rising Sun pub — one of many pubs of merit in the village.

Continue across Coltishall Lower Common, a popular mooring point for Broads cruisers, where the ducks are always hungry, and the views are unspoilt. At the end of the common, take the small road running parallel with the river heading towards a brick and flint wall, past the Old Rectory house, and a 'Dead End' sign. At the lane's end, be sure to notice, on the left, the sweetest cottages that Norfolk can boast. This is Anchor Street, once famous for its boat building.

ℹ *Coltishall is reputed to have been the birthplace of the wherry. It is believed that keels, the forerunners of the wherries, were built in Coltishall, but the place emerged as a major wherry building centre in the second half of the 19th century after John Allen bought a boatyard in Anchor Street for £400. With a team of skilled boat builders the yard turned out an average of one new wherry every year from the 1860s to the turn of the century. But not only were they productive, Allens built the fastest wherries in Norfolk. Their long slender, sleek lines were built especially for the narrow waters of the Ant and the Bure.*

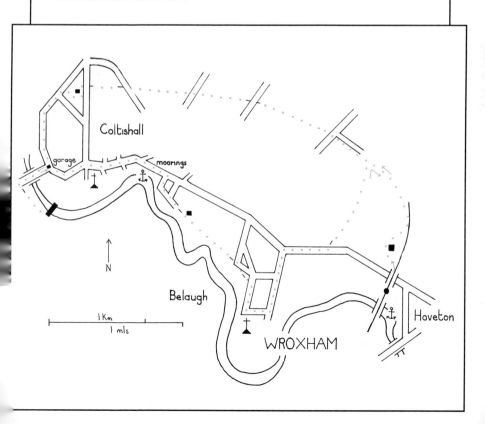

Local historian, Richard Bond, in his book Coltishall. *Heyday of a Broadland Village, describes the boat builders of Anchor Street as the aristocrats of labour, who having served a strict seven-year apprenticeship, emerged as an elite band of artisans.*

"Working from dawn till dusk in an organised chaos of crumbling workshops, lean-to paint sheds and rat-ridden wood piles, the village boat builders were a unique occupational community. They built and repaired wherries with near religious devotion, jealously guarding the reputation of their yard."

Wherries were built without plans or drawings. Huge oak trees were felled from local estates and hauled to the boatyard saw-pit. Every part of the wherry, from tabernacle to tiller was hand-made. The last wherry built in Norfolk, the Ella *was launched at Coltishall in 1912, but Allens, like other boatyards, quickly diversified to produce new craft, such as wherry yachts for pleasure cruising. After the First World War the yard maintained the wherries which still sailed the waterways, and later built and hired out Broads cruisers. The end came in 1974 when the yard was sold, the boat sheds unceremoniously demolished to make way for a modern residential development. Sadly not one of the Allens' wherries remains as a testament to the skill of the Coltishall craftsmen.*

The public footpath sign leads you along the edge of the next field, with the river on the right. Cross the stile into the next field and you feel you are in a piece of forgotten rural England. A pastoral idyll, with the natural sweep of the field down to the river on the right, and ahead, the beckoning tower of Belaugh church. Over another stile into the next field and the mighty oaks on the left complete the rural patchwork. The field narrows; cross another stile to a small loke, which passes between a converted barn on the left and a brick and flint house on the right. Fork right through the kissing gate across a small field, where coots graze at the river's edge, and cross yet another stile to leave the field and join a small road, turning right towards the church and the buildings of Belaugh.

The river frontages are suddenly more tidied and manicured than the wild, unkept riverside left behind. This tiny village too has its staithe, or parish land point, and its boatyards. Climb the hill towards St Peters Church, Belaugh, a tiny building, quite in keeping with the scale of the rest of the village. Broads holidaymakers can be assured of a warm welcome here. Its whitewashed walls and tiny pews are immaculate, and the care and industry which has been invested in the imaginative set of kneelers says much about the love local people have for the church.

Leave the church the way you came, turning right onto the road, up a slight hill to a T-junction. Turn left here and follow this road until it joins the B1354. Turn right towards Wroxham and Hoveton. This next leg is perhaps the least pleasant of the route, and walkers should be wary of drivers travelling too fast along this narrow country lane. You will pass a house on the right called The Gables. About 50 metres on the

Maintaining rights of way. Area Countryside Officer, Declan Keiley, puts the finishing touches to a Broads Authority stile on a wet winter morning.

left after this is a public footpath sign pointing through the hedge. This path follows the line of a hedgerow bisecting two fields. At the end of the field, cut through the gap and turn right, following the edge of the next field. At the top of the field, turn left and head towards the railway embankment. Climb the wooden steps and you are back on the Bure Valley Walk. Turn right and walk the short distance back to Hoveton and Wroxham.

When you reach Wroxham again it is worth continuing into Wroxham and Hoveton villages. Leave the station car park and take the first right. This leads to the centre of the village, passing the Broads Information Centre on the right. At the cross-roads, turn right to reach the bridge over the Bure. A walkway is on the left-hand side and from here is a good vantage point to watch the holiday river traffic.

i *It was really here that it all began with one John Loynes, the pioneer of the Broads cruising holiday, who founded the famous boat builders, J Loynes and Sons Ltd.*

His love of sailing had started when he taught himself to sail in a small lugsail dinghy belonging to the estate on which he was working. He later set up in business as a carpenter in Norwich, and he discovered in the workshop that he had hired an old rotting rowing boat. He bought it cheaply and took it apart, numbering every piece, and then working in his spare time, painstakingly rebuilt it. News that this 14ft craft was for hire soon spread around the city, and Loynes realised it was worth building another from scratch. This he did with the aid of some old plans, making the mast, spars and oars himself, as well as shaping and stitching the sails.

Day boats for hire at Wroxham

Interest grew, and then in the early 1880s he produced what was probably the first guide to the Broads issued by a boat-letting firm. In it he advertised "A good selection of cruising boats", from 13 – 20 ft in length, ready to be collected from Norwich or Wroxham. And it added: "Instruction in sailing given."

It was the start of greater things. John recognised the strategic importance of Wroxham and soon set up a yard close by the bridge. Three of his sons joined him in business and as well as hiring boats they also ran mini-cruises for day trippers. After the First World War the demand for boat lettings increased and Blake's started to act as agents for several firms — the hire boat industry had begun.

Day boats by the score can today be hired from Wroxham, and from here is it possible to explore down river to Hoveton Great Broad where there is a fascinating nature trail.

Useful addresses

British Rail. Tel: Norwich (0603) 632055.

Norfolk Bus Information Centre for information about all bus services including the Sunday Explorer service along the North Norfolk coast. Tel: Norwich (0603) 613613.

North Norfolk Railway, Sheringham Station. Tel: (0263) 822045. Talking Timetable (0263) 825449.

Bure Valley Railway, The Old Station, Norwich Road, Aylsham. Tel: (0263) 733858.

Broads Authority, Thomas Harvey House, 18 Colegate, Norwich. Tel: (0603) 610734.

Broads Authority Information Centres at:

Hoveton/Wroxham: Station Road, Hoveton, Norwich. Tel: (0603) 782281.

Ranworth: The Staithe, Ranworth, Norwich. Tel: (060 549) 453.

Beccles: The Quay, Fen Lane, Beccles. Tel: (0502) 713196.

Toad Hole Cottage Museum: How Hill, Ludham. Tel: (069 262) 763.

North West Tower, Great Yarmouth. Tel: (0493) 332095.

Norwich Tourist Information, The Guildhall, Norwich. Tel: (0603) 666071.

Norfolk Naturalists Trust, 72, Cathedral Close, Norwich. Tel: (0603) 625540.

Suffolk Wildlife Trust, Carlton Marshes Nature Reserve. Tel: (0502) 564250.

Cromer Museum, East Cottages, Tucker Street, Cromer. Tel: (0263) 513543.

Norfolk Coast Project, 6 Station Road, Wells-next-the-Sea, Norfolk. Tel: (0328) 711533.

Tunstall Camping Barn. Tel: (0493) 700279.

The National Trust. Regional Office. Tel: (0263) 733471.

THE BROADS
Britain's finest wetland on your doorstep

photography : Richard Denyer

Information Centres

Open : Easter - October

Station Road, Hoveton.
Tel (0603) 782281

The Staithe, Ranworth.
Tel (060 549) 453

The Quay, Fen Lane,
Beccles.
Tel (0502) 713196

North West Tower,
North Quay,
Gt.Yarmouth.
Tel (0493) 332095

Toad Hole Cottage
Museum and Wildlife
Water Trail, How Hill,
Ludham.
Tel (069 262) 763

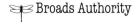 Broads Authority